The Pocket
Small Business
Owner's Guide to
Building Your
Business

Kevin Devine

ALLWORTH PRESS
NEW YORK

Allworth Press books may be purchased in bulk at special discounts for sales promotion, corporate gifts, fund-raising, or educational purposes. Special editions can also be created to specifications. For details, contact the Special Sales Department, Allworth Press, 307 West 36th Street, 11th Floor, New York, NY 10018 or info@skyhorsepublishing.com.

15 14 13 12 11   5 4 3 2 1

Published by Allworth Press
An imprint of Skyhorse Publishing
307 West 36th Street, 11th Floor, New York, NY 10018.

Allworth Press® is a registered trademark of Skyhorse Publishing, Inc.®, a Delaware corporation.

www.allworth.com

Cover design by Brian Peterson

ISBN: 978-1-58115-902-8

Library of Congress Cataloging-in-Publication Data is available on file.

Printed in the United States of America.

This book is dedicated to Eunice and Jo, two women who showed me that being able to help others is the highest honor.

Table of Contents

Table of Contents

Introduction

How This Book Can Help You

For years I have helped people from all walks of life to improve their lives through self-employment. Many of these folks had been laid off or had barriers that prevented them from working full time. Some others were just interested in starting a business and were curious about what they needed to know.

Teaching these program participants, and helping former participants who went on to start businesses, I learned all the little details that business owners need to know. Time and again participants told me, "I didn't know there was so much to know!" There is a lot to know, and this book contains much of it. Reading this book will give you a tremendous leg up on getting your business started the right way.

However, this book is not designed to make you an expert in every task you'll need to accomplish to successfully run your business. As we'll see, you should be an expert in two things: what it is your business does and how to provide excellent customer service. Most of the other things you do not need to know in detail, but you should still be familiar with.

It's like owning and driving a car; you should have an idea of how it works, or at least the good sense to know who to call if something is wrong. You certainly don't need to know how to change the spark plugs; you can pay someone else to do that.

In the same way, this book presents the basic information you need to know to run a business, describes how to find and use other resources, and helps you to have the common sense to know when things are going wrong.

How to Use This Book

This book is designed to be a learning tool. Read it carefully and completely. It would be best if you read it from start to finish, as the later chapters assume you know what is in the earlier ones, but this is not essential.

Keeping Track of Your Progress

This book is written so that the information is presented in about the same order as you'll need to know it as you start your business. For example, we discuss legal business entities near the front, because you should decide that before going much further. You can also pick and choose chapters to get just the information you need.

There is a brief checklist on page 236 of the steps that nearly all businesses will have to complete as they start. Note that you will be in a much better position to complete these tasks after you have completed this book.

Each chapter ends with a section called Nail It Down! This section has practical points you should know, and steps you should take, to start a successful business. Also included are references to additional resources to help you learn more.

Be sure to go through this section carefully when you have finished a chapter to make sure you have a thorough understanding of the topic.

Nail It Down!

Use the Nail It Down! section to keep track of your progress, or as a review for what you learned in each chapter. To get the most out of this book, follow these suggestions:

❑ Set aside some time each day to use this book.

❑ Seek out other resources such as the Small Business Development Center for classes and assistance.

❑ Track your progress by checking off the steps in the Nail It Down! section.

Chapter One

Know Yourself and Your Business

N ot everyone is cut out to be self-employed. If running a business was easy, we would all do it! But the fact is that most people who can work choose to work for someone else. About 90 percent of the workforce is employed by a business owned by someone else. Less than 10 percent rely on self-employment income.

To know whether or not you can be successful in your own business, it pays to have a good handle on why you want to be in business, what your strengths are, and what your business is all about. That way, you will be in a better position to decide whether or not starting a business is right for you.

Why Be in Business?

Why do you want to start a business? Take a second and write down the three main reasons.

❶ _____

❷ _____

❸ _____

In the years I've taught classes to people like you who want to start solo businesses (what I call business run by one, maybe two, people), here are the most common reasons I have heard for wanting to start a business:

- More free time
- Financial independence
- Be my own boss

I'm guessing that at least two of the three reasons you gave match these three. It is true that if you want to be really rich, with the opportunity to have lots of free time and make your own decisions, owning a business is one of the best ways to accomplish these goals.

But because this book is about the things that you need to know before you start a business, here are some things to keep in mind:

- Most people who own a business work many more hours than those who work for someone else.

- Many small business owners earn less, sometimes much less, than those who work for someone else. Some will lose so much they declare bankruptcy.

- You are never your own boss. While you get to decide many details of how your

business runs, it is always in the service of
your customers, who are your true bosses.

These facts are not meant to scare you. Rather, they are
meant to open your eyes. Keep this in mind if you are considering starting a business: Unless you do it right, starting a
business can make your life worse than it is now. You don't
want that. I don't want that either, which is one reason why
I wrote this book.

Starting and running a business isn't easy. Not only have I
run a business myself, I've worked in a mom-and-pop business
that went belly-up, and I've had lots of experience helping others explore their business dreams. If there is anything I have
learned, it is that starting a business can either be the best thing
you have ever done, or it can ruin your life. The rest of this
chapter can help you decide which path is right for you.

How to Improve Your Odds

Too many people who start a business overestimate their
ability. They think that because they see others apparently
making it without much trouble that they can do it as well.
What they don't realize is that only the success stories make
the news. The numerous failures are ignored. But you know
many will sink instead of swim.

What might be some ways to help improve your odds of
success? Take a second and think about it.

Learn, Learn, Learn
No one gets to be an expert in any field without first learning
what there is to know. Your odds of success skyrocket if you
first learn about what mistakes to avoid and discover what
you need to know to steer clear of failure. For running a
business this means reading books, taking classes, and talking to existing business owners.

Practice, Practice, Practice

Second in importance is to practice. For running a business, that means actually working in the industry for someone else before starting your own business, or at least keeping your operation part-time until it can support you.

Get Help

Third, it isn't cheating to get some help. No small business succeeds without relying on the professional advice and service of others. Most communities have a variety of resources such as Small Business Development Centers (SBDCs; http://www.sba.gov), Senior Corp of Retired Executives offices (SCORE; http://www.score.org), or other nonprofit organizations that offer training and advice to small business owners. Organizations that are supported by the Small Business Administration (SBA; http://www.sba.gov) or other government programs are unbiased and won't try to sell you anything.

Have a Backup

Finally, it can't hurt to have a backup plan. In business, this means (and you should commit this phrase to memory) don't quit your day job! The day job, whether it is a full-time, part-time, or a secondary source of income, can actually make your chance of business success more likely, since it can provide income even when your business is slow.

Sometimes people get really excited about starting a business and can't wait to get going. This is understandable, and I've felt that rush of excitement myself. But as we'll discuss later, getting ideas is easy; actually doing the work is tough.

Starting a business, like any career, takes time. Keep your day job and take things one step at a time.

Your Strengths and Weaknesses

Part of knowing yourself means knowing what it is that you can and cannot do yourself. Running a business makes you feel great; you are establishing your independence and showing the world that you can stand on your own. And yet, even if you could perform all of the tasks that a business requires, you would be foolish to try.

What Can You Handle Yourself?

Here is a partial list of all of the things that every business has to do. Check off those that you think you can handle by yourself:

- ❑ Have a product to sell
- ❑ Find the market for your product
- ❑ Market and sell that product
- ❑ Actually perform the work (make the product or provide the service)
- ❑ Bookkeeping and accounting (including taxes)
- ❑ Manage the business, including yourself
- ❑ Manage employees (if you have them)
- ❑ Work the computer (if you use one)

Most people realize that they can't handle all of these responsibilities well enough for their business to succeed. And even if you could, you wouldn't want to because you won't have the time.

Getting the Work Done

So what can you do to make sure that all of these tasks get completed? Here are some ideas.

Learn What You Need

First, you could educate yourself, perhaps by taking a course. This is especially true if you don't need that much help. For example, if you are good with numbers but don't know anything about bookkeeping, a community-college class might be all you need to handle your own books. Or maybe you have some management experience but aren't familiar with payroll laws; reading IRS publications may get you on your way.

Get Outside Help

Second, you could have others help you with your weaknesses, either as employees, partners, or business associates. There are advantages and disadvantages to all of these, but it is fairly common for two people to get together who have complementary strengths and weaknesses to form a team that is better than either one alone.

You could also hire out some of this work. In fact, many solo businesses these days are professionals like you who provide bookkeeping, computer, or marketing services to other small businesses.

Get Around the Barrier

Finally, for some of these tasks, you can just arrange your business so that you don't have to do them at all. This is especially true if you don't need employees or a computer. Many businesses get by very well without either one.

KNOW YOUR BUSINESS

Have you told anyone about your business idea? If so, what did you say? Were you able to explain it to them quickly, in a few dozen words or less? Or did you have to go on and on because they couldn't seem to understand what you were getting at?

In this section, you will think about and write out your mission statement, a brief description of your business that outlines what it sells and what it means to you.

Your Business Foundation

Every building needs a foundation. Buildings without foundations are only as secure as the changing environment around them. They are susceptible to wind, storms, and changes in the landscape that buildings with strong foundations can easily resist.

Your business should have a strong foundation. For many businesses, that foundation can be a mission statement. Mission statements are brief descriptions of your business that define, in very broad terms, what your business is all about and what you want to get out of it.

Often solo business owners will get so caught up in the day-to-day running of their businesses that they have a hard time seeing the forest for the trees. They have difficulty making decisions because they can't isolate the important issues. Mission statements give you a way of seeing the "big picture," helping you decide what your business should be.

Mission statements reflect you and your values. They provide a way for you to put into words what your business is about. That way, when things get hectic and decisions need to be made, you can examine your mission statement, and reflect on what road you should take.

Mission statements are written by you and for you. They are primarily intended to be used within your business, not shared with customers. That means that mission statements do not include slogans or marketing hype. But they must take into account who your customers are, because your customers are your business.

Mission statements can be difficult to write because they ask you to think about the big picture, to envision the broad goals that most of us simply are not used to thinking about. You have to establish the groundwork for your business before you can build. The mission statement will be your foundation.

What Is My Business All About?

What I would like you to do now is write down exactly what your business idea is, as briefly as you can. Mention these things:

- What you sell (products or services)
- Who your primary customers will be
- Where you will be located
- What sets your business apart
- What values are important to you

If you have trouble explaining your idea, chances are it is because:

- Your idea really is complex and it takes a lot of words to describe it, or
- you are having trouble describing your business in an efficient way, or
- you really are not sure what your business idea is.

If you think you are simply having trouble describing your business, try it again. See if you can reduce the number of words in your description. Write out your description and give it to someone else to see if they understand it.

If your only problem was actually finding the words to describe your business, we can solve that. The bigger problem is that, if you can't explain what your business is all about, maybe you don't really know.

The Thirty-Word Rule

How long should your mission statement be? One rule of thumb is that you should be able to give a thorough description in thirty words or less. You might want to try writing down your business description again, using fewer but more expressive words.

If you are still having problems, it is probably because you really don't know what your business idea is. Your dream is still too vague to put into words, kind of like an image that is still too fuzzy to draw on paper. An excellent way for you to help solidify your business idea would be to just read through this book. Then, once you have an idea of what you'll need to know, you can come back to this chapter and start again.

You Have to Know, Really Know, Your Business

Your mission statement is designed to give you the big picture, the "in a nutshell" purpose and goal for your business. But it is only a starting point. It really isn't good enough to have a vague idea, to have some general notions, about your business. A mission statement is an excellent starting place, but if you want to be successful you have to be more specific.

To really plan a successful business you'll have to be able to answer some of the nitty-gritty questions about the details of running your business (writing a business plan will force you to confront these questions). Someone who has only dreamed of starting a business can write a mission statement, but only someone who is serious and has spent a lot of time thinking about his or her idea can write a complete business description.

Let's go back to our house-construction example. Let's say that the mission statement for our house was, "To have a bright, open house that is energy efficient and built to last." It sounds like a nice house, but where do the doors go? How large will the garage be? How many bedrooms?

As you can see, the mission statement doesn't do much to answer the detailed questions—the what, where, and how questions that any builder would need to have answered to construct the house.

In the same way, having a general business idea in mind isn't bad for your initial planning, but you must narrow down your idea if you want to save time and money. This book will provide the fundamental knowledge you need to help clarify your business idea. Completing the Nail It Down! sections will help make your ideas concrete, and writing a business plan will finish the job.

Can Your Business Stand on Its Own?

You've had a chance to think about how your particular strengths and weaknesses match up with the demands of your business idea. Now let's see if you can leverage your strengths into business success.

A little earlier I identified eight essential business tasks that all business owners must complete. To simplify things a little we can combine those tasks into three fundamental elements. These three elements are:

- The product or the work
- Sales and marketing
- Management (of yourself, your employees, and money)

Think about it this way. Your business is like a three-legged stool. These three elements form the legs upon which your business success stands. If any one of them is weak or fails, the whole business falls to the ground. It doesn't really matter if your product is the best in the market, or your quality is unequaled. If you can't manage the business, or market successfully and find customers, you will not succeed. A stool cannot stand on one or two legs.

*Your business success depends upon the support of
all three essential elements*

Your Strengths Will Support You . . .

Most people who start a small business come into the business because they have a special expertise or knowledge that they can sell. In nearly every business, doing the work is the easy part, because that's what brings the owner to the business in the first place.

But Your Weaknesses Will Defeat You

Most solo businesses that fail do so because the owner neglected their weaknesses, not their strengths. In my time helping others start their businesses, I have yet to see one fail because the owner couldn't do the work. It was always due to a lack of sales, marketing, or a failure to manage themselves, their employees, or their money.

In the chapters that follow, we'll look at each of these three essential elements, and how you can make sure that your business stool stands on three strong legs.

Making the Best Decision for You

Part of the goal of this book is to give you the information you need to make an informed, reasonable decision as to which path to take. You might decide that your business idea is a good one, and that you have the capacity to start your business now. This book should definitely help you learn what you need to be a success.

Many will decide that, while their business idea is a good one, they are not yet ready to start their business. Perhaps they need some more education, to save more money, or to get more work experience.

Finally, you may decide that running a business isn't for you. As we've seen, most people don't run their own businesses, and for good reason.

Here is the important point: Any of these decisions can be the right one for you. You are the best person to make this decision, and you don't have to do it now. Keep reading this book, learn all you can, and we'll talk more about the future at the end of the book.

Nail It Down!

Here are some of the questions you'll have to answer as you proceed with planning your business. If you are still in the planning stages, you may not know the answers to all of these questions yet (we'll be exploring many of them in upcoming chapters). If you have already started doing business, you'll either know the answers to these questions, or you'll be discovering the answers the hard way soon enough!

❑ What is your business name? Who owns the business?

❑ What is the legal entity of the business?

❑ What do you make or sell? What is your product?

❑ What is your role in the business? What qualifies you to take on these roles?

❑ What benefits does the customer realize by buying or using your product?

❑ What sets your business apart from the competition? What is your competitive edge?

❑ Who are your customers? Where do they live? How much money do they make? What are their hobbies?

❑ What are your general marketing ideas? What kind of a budget do you have for marketing?

❑ What are the one-year and three-year goals of your business?

❑ Which of these suggestions should you take while getting your business off the ground?

    ❑ Take lessons (read books, take classes, etc.)

    ❑ Practice (run your business on the side or work for someone else in the industry)

    ❑ Get professional advice (seek out the SBDC, SCORE, or other nonprofits that offer classes and assistance)

    ❑ Have a life preserver (keep your day job)

❑ What additional skills should you develop as you prepare to start your business?

Chapter Two

KNOW THE FOUR STEPS TO SUCCESS

I f you are reading this book, it means that you are serious about running a business, and serious about doing it right. The steps I will outline here are not the only way you can think about starting a business, but it is a process that works, and I would encourage you to study it, use it, and adapt it to your needs.

STEP ONE: THE IDEA

Everything that someone will do starts with an idea. Whether you're going to throw a birthday party, go to the store, or build the tallest building in the world, you have to picture it first in your mind.

Ideas Are Easy
But let's face it—ideas are easy. Many people come up with ideas all of the time for inventions, books, or businesses. But

how many of them actually carry out these plans? Very few, because the next steps after the idea are much harder.

Ideas should provide you with a vision of what you want to accomplish, a goal you want to achieve. Ideas won't be meaningful to you unless they are realistic and achievable.

Ideas have to generate action before they can become real.

Ideas Are Only the First of Several Steps

Many people make the mistake of going right from having an idea to trying to act on that idea, without first planning how they will accomplish the action. I would suggest that after establishing your business idea you should not act but should plan actions based on your idea. Think of it this way: A football team has the idea to score a touchdown. But without a plan, how do they know what to do?

STEP TWO: THE PLAN

Before you can take action to achieve your goal, you should plan on exactly how you are going to do it. But many of us don't make plans before we take action, we just get an idea and act on it. Why? There are two reasons I can think of.

Planning Isn't Automatic

You're probably thinking, I usually don't make plans, I just do things. Most of us don't consciously plan to do things like go to the store, we just do them. Kind of like walking or breathing—for most of us we just skip the planning because these activities are second nature. Think back, though, to the first time you did something new, like driving a car or using a computer. Chances are you had to do things very slowly, one step at a time, and you had to think about each step as you went. When you haven't done something before it takes significantly more work.

So, if you haven't started a business before, it would only make sense that you treat it the same way you treated that first time at the wheel or in front of the computer: by going slowly, planning what you want to do before you do it, and only then acting on your plan.

Planning Can Be Tough

The second reason planning is so often overlooked is that planning can be scary. Taking on any new challenge can be intimidating. The steps can be too large, the barriers too big, to think about how you are going to overcome them. Faced with this dilemma, I've seen some people freeze, unable to go forward, while others just take a blind leap. Unfortunately, both options often lead to failure.

I would suggest to you that those are the exact reasons you should plan your actions, and your business. It is better, easier, and cheaper to fail in the planning stages than for real.

Planning Can Make Things Easier

Consider how you can make the scary planning process a little easier. That would be by not taking it on all at once. Small steps are easy, but they add up. When I first approach writing a book, I am always intimidated. I think to myself, how will I ever write 200 pages? That is so much! But then I set myself smaller goals. I don't need to write 200 pages, I only need to write one page. And if that page looks too intimidating, I just remember that I don't have to write a page, I just have to write a sentence. Soon the words begin to form sentences, the sentences form pages, and 200 pages later, I have my book.

Planning for your business should entail creating a business plan. Tools available to help you with your plan include software, books, and consulting, any of which can help you break down the process of writing a business plan into small, easy-to-tackle steps.

Step Three: Take Action

Once you have a plan in place, you are ready to take action. Skipping the planning stage gets people into trouble.

When your action follows your plan you can know exactly where you are, where you are going, and how you can get there. Without the plan, you are lost.

You might think that taking action is the last step in your journey to success, but it isn't.

Step Four: Evaluation

As long as you only do something once, you don't have to evaluate how well you did it. You'll never get the chance to do it again, so what difference does it make? But most things you do in life you do repeatedly, and your business is an excellent example. Even though you may only start a business once, many of your initial decisions and actions will be repeated over and over, such as the purchase of materials, how you distribute your product, the hours that you will work, and so on. Each of these areas is ripe for improvement, and the only way you can improve is by evaluating how well your action helped achieve your goal, and to come up with a new idea and plan for changing the action to better meet your goal the next time.

This is one reason why starting a business on the side (that is, keeping the day job), has been the key to success for many business owners. Starting small allowed them to make mistakes and learn the ropes when not much was at stake, so they could learn which ideas worked and which didn't.

Nail It Down!

We'll discuss some more specific planning strategies in chapter 12, *Know How to Manage Your Business*. In the meantime, here are some concrete planning steps you can take now:

❑ Make sure your business idea is reasonable and well thought out.

❑ Begin planning for how you will turn your ideas into reality.

   ❑ Complete reading this book.

   ❑ Work through the exercises and checklists.

   ❑ Begin working on a business plan.

❑ Put your plan into action.

❑ Regularly evaluate your ideas, plans, and actions, and adjust accordingly.

KNOW YOUR LEGAL ENTITY

W hen you start your business, it will have certain rights and obligations depending on the legal entity you pick for the business. The legal entity is how the law deals with your business for legal, regulatory, and sometimes tax considerations.

IMPACTS OF YOUR LEGAL ENTITY

There are several factors you need to consider when deciding on the legal entity you want your business to have. These factors are:

- Control: Do you want to have absolute control over your business, or are you willing to share the decision-making with others?

- Liability: As a business owner, you put your assets (what you own) at risk. Your business entity can help protect some of your assets if you are sued or have financial trouble.

- Adapting to changes: Do you want to be able to make changes quickly, or are you happy to let the business find its own way?

- Taxes: Your legal entity may or may not be significant from a tax viewpoint. In some cases it may make no difference, and in others it may make a large difference. Your entity certainly can affect how complex your taxes will be to calculate, and perhaps how much you owe.

In this chapter, we'll look at how each of these factors affects each of the different legal entities. We'll start with the simplest form of business and move toward the most complicated. Each entity has advantages and disadvantages, and no one form is right for every business.

SOLE PROPRIETOR

The simplest, and most common, type of business entity is the sole proprietorship. "Sole proprietor" literally means "one owner," and that's exactly what a sole proprietor is. In a sole proprietorship, you are the business. That is, there is no separation, for legal or tax purposes, between you personally and the business. Sole proprietors can have employees, and the businesses that they run can be of any size, but many are one- or two-person operations.

Control and Liability
From a legal perspective, sole proprietors do not own a business, they simply do business. Sole proprietors do, however, own the business's assets and liabilities, so business assets are also personal assets, and business liabilities are also personal liabilities. (Assets are things you own that have value, and liabilities are debts you owe. We'll talk

about assets and liabilities in much more detail in chapter 14, *Know Accounting Basics.*) Sole proprietors have complete control over the business and also assume all the responsibility for the business.

This means the proprietor has complete control over what the business does and how it is run, but also means that if the business goes into debt, the creditors (to whom you owe money) are allowed to try and seek repayment from your personal assets. This would include your car, your boat, and your house. In a sole proprietorship, business assets and liabilities are also personal assets and liabilities.

There are two situations where a creditor may seek your personal assets to satisfy a business debt. The first is if, in the course of your business, someone is hurt as a result of doing business with you and sues you to recover damages. This is called a tort. For example, a customer might slip and fall in your place of business, or if you cause an auto accident while on business. Your first line of defense against torts should always be to carry liability insurance. (I'll explain a lot more about insurance in the chapter 4, *Know Who Will Help You*).

The second situation would be if your business runs up debts that the business cannot pay back. You can't buy insurance against bad business decisions. So if you take a risk and buy much more in inventory than you are able to sell before the supplier demands payment, you may find yourself so far in debt you can't get out. Obviously you'll have to liquidate your business assets, and if those are not enough to satisfy your creditors, you will then have to sell your personal assets as well.

Adapting to Changes

Being the only owner of a sole proprietorship means that you have the ability to change your business in any way you want at any time you want. You can start and stop business at any time, keeping in mind that there may be tax and regulatory paperwork to be done, but no business entity is more flexible.

Taxes

Sole proprietorship taxes are as simple as business taxes get, although for many businesses taxes are never simple. Sole proprietorships are considered "pass-through" business entities for tax purposes. This means that the business profits and losses are reported and paid (or lost) on the proprietor's personal tax forms. The business itself does not file a tax return, because in a sole proprietorship there is no business separate from the owner. For tax purposes, the sole proprietor keeps track of business and personal finances separately, reports the business income and expenses on a Schedule C, Net Profit from Business, and then carries that result over to his or her Form 1040 individual tax return. Obviously if you have an inventory and employees the tax situation gets more complicated, but if not, this is as simple as it gets. (We'll go into much more detail about taxes in a sole proprietorship in chapter 15, *Know How to Minimize Your Taxes.*)

Pros and Cons

Simple to Set Up

Most states have no legal requirements to establish a sole proprietorship other than obtaining the proper licenses and paying taxes. This makes starting and stopping business very easy. For example, if you run a part-time business out of your home, perhaps selling cosmetics or kitchen goods, your risk is low and it may be more work than it is worth to do anything other than establish a sole proprietorship.

Complete Liability

Although a sole proprietor gets to keep all of the profits of the business, many potential proprietors are rightly concerned with the potential liability they face. Sole proprietors have complete liability for the business, and that is the largest drawback to this form of business. The more you have, the more you have to lose by starting a sole proprietorship.

Can you start your business as a sole proprietor and upgrade at a later date? Yes, although in most states starting a Limited Liability Company (LLC) is so easy that many professionals discourage proprietorships and encourage LLCs, even for the smallest businesses (we'll discuss LLCs in detail shortly).

Potential Trap for Spouses

Another potential drawback is that the spouse of a sole proprietor may be liable for business debts, especially if he or she helps out the business in any way. If the proprietor takes the business into debt and then dies, the creditors may then come after the surviving spouse claiming that he or she is now the proprietor. If you have a sole proprietorship and your spouse doesn't want the responsibility of running the business if you should die, your easiest option is to form an LLC, or to write up a contract excluding them from inheriting the business. How the law treats this situation varies somewhat from state to state, so you might want to check out the law in your state before starting your sole proprietorship.

Is Sole Proprietorship Right for Me?

A sole proprietorship may be the best business entity for you if:

- Your business is very low risk.

- You will carry plenty of insurance.

- You have few personal assets to protect.

- You really hate any paperwork.

- You will be in business for a very short time.

Partnership

When two or more people go into business together, they often form a partnership. Like a marriage, partnerships have their advantages and disadvantages. And, like a marriage, the partnership may be stronger than two separate individuals because the owners may have complementary strengths.

But partnerships are also potentially dangerous. Just as when a marriage goes sour each partner can incur substantial costs and be left worse off than before, so in a business partnership the partners can lose more than they bargained for if the partnership goes sour. Some of these problems can be avoided by structuring the partnership correctly and by planning on how the partnership will end.

Control

Any time two or more people get together to make decisions, disputes can erupt. If you are considering a partnership, think about what will happen if you and your partners disagree, one decides to end the partnership, or one dies. Sometimes one partner will want out of the partnership for perfectly understandable reasons, but the other partner doesn't want to let them out. I worked with two young women who ran a successful hair salon. One became pregnant and wanted to leave the partnership to be a full-time mother. The other didn't want to let her out. What can they do?

Plan the Divorce Before the Marriage

Experts recommend that if you form a partnership, you should plan the divorce before you get married. Plan for how the partnership will end and what steps you will take to let a partner go. Will the other partners buy them out? If so, for how much? What happens if one partner wants the other to leave? What happens if one partner dies? These issues can get terribly complicated very quickly.

Luckily, many partnerships have run into these issues before and many small business attorneys have experience drafting partnership agreements that spell out, in writing, the answers to these questions. These documents, often called "buy-sell" agreements because they explain how one partner will buy out the other, are kind of like prenuptial agreements in a marriage. If you are thinking about a partnership, you should have a partnership agreement so that you know the answer to such questions as:

- Who is responsible for what work?

- How will the profits and losses be divided?

- What happens if the partners choose to split?

- What happens if one partner dies?

As with all contracts, the point of a partnership agreement isn't to prove your case in court, it is to prevent the need to go to court in the first place. By planning for the worst, you are prepared in the event the worst happens.

Liability

The liability you face in a partnership depends largely on the form of partnership your business has. Partnerships can be structured in a variety of ways, and different states may handle partnerships differently. The first type, a general partnership, is much like two sole proprietors working together. General partnerships, like sole proprietors, are unregulated by the states, and each partner may have complete responsibility for all of the business debt. The legal term for this arrangement, joint and several liability, means that all of the partners are individually and jointly responsible for the business. For example, if in a general partnership one partner goes on a spending spree using the company's checkbook and then that partner leaves town, the other partners may be responsible for all of the debt.

Note that general partnerships are not legal entities (that is, the state does not regulate them), and because of this, many sole proprietors working together may be considered general partners without realizing it.

The second common type of partnership is a limited partnership. These partnerships, which are registered with the state, do not have the joint-and-several-liability problem of general partnerships. Instead, each partner is only responsible for his or her investment in the business. You can only lose what you put in. These partnerships are legal entities and the business has legal status.

Adapting to Changes
Obviously one of the potential drawbacks for any partnership is the difficulty in making changes to the business when the partners disagree. The best advice here is to draw up a written partnership agreement.

Taxes
Taxes for most partnerships are relatively straightforward. Partnerships are usually handled as "pass-through" business entities for tax purposes. This means that the business profits and losses are reported and paid (or lost) on each of the partner's personal tax forms. In addition, the partnership entity will have to file a form reporting the business income or loss, but it does not pay taxes itself. You'll probably benefit from getting help with partnership taxes.

Pros and Cons
If you have a great business idea but lack the expertise or financial resources to get the business off the ground, a partnership might be the way to go. Working together, many

business owners have accomplished more than they would have working apart.

But, most partnerships will one day end. How your partnership ends is really up to you. If you fail to plan for it, chances are very good that it will end poorly. But with proper planning, it can end smoothly. Helping you do this planning is something that many small business attorneys specialize in.

Is a Partnership Right for Me?

A partnership may be the best business entity for you if:

- You need the experience, help, or financial backing of a partner.

- You can work well with others.

- You are willing to negotiate how the business will dissolve before it starts.

Limited Liability Company (LLC)

In the 1980s and 1990s, many states created a new business entity to help the growing number of small businesses. Business owners wanted more legal protection than they could achieve with a sole proprietorship, but didn't want all of the legal hassles involved with creating a corporation (as we'll see later, corporations are the most complex of legal entities). So states created a hybrid, or intermediate, legal entity called a Limited Liability Company, or LLC.

LLCs create a legal barrier between you as an individual (you and your personal assets) and your business (and its assets). This gives small business owners more legal protection than they would have operating as sole proprietors.

Control

An LLC can be owned by one or more individuals, who are called members. Unlike a sole proprietor, a single-member LLC owner is not his or her business; he or she is the sole member of the business. As such, the sole member is free to control his or her business just as much as a sole proprietor. In fact, in many ways, a single-member LLC operates exactly like a sole proprietorship, and this is a good example.

Multimember LLCs are very much like partnerships, although they have some advantages over general partnerships. First, there is no joint and several liability in an LLC, so each member's liability is limited to his or her investment. Second, it would be rare that a spouse would be considered a "silent" member of the LLC unless they invested substantially in the business. Finally, because LLCs are legal entities, it is clear that multimember LLCs are partnerships and not just some people working together.

However, some of the pitfalls of partnerships can also apply to multimember LLCs. The members may still disagree, some of them may want to pull out, and so on. It is still a good idea to discuss these problems ahead of time and put your decisions in writing.

Liability

The main reason states created LLCs was to establish additional legal protection for small business owners. The LLC concept puts a legal barrier or shield between the assets of the business and the personal assets of the members. In an LLC, the law recognizes that the business owner is separate from the business, and the owner's personal assets are separate from the business assets. This means that if the business is sued, only the business assets are at risk. Remember, regardless of your business, you want to have insurance to cover whatever risk you face due to accidents, but you can't get insurance against your own bad business decisions. If your business goes into debt due to your poor judgment, and you have an LLC, the law will help protect your personal assets.

Maintaining Your LLC Protection

In return for the protection the law provides your personal assets in an LLC, it requires that you follow certain rules. These rules are designed to help ensure that those you do business with understand that they are doing business with a business and not with you as an individual. There are three things that you can do to help ensure the law protects you.

- The LLC protection is strongest when the owner does not casually mix personal assets with business assets, so keep personal and business assets separate. This doesn't mean that you can't put personal assets into the business; you are expected to do this. But you must make sure that the business expenses are paid with business checks, personal expenses are paid with personal checks, and that any transfers between the two are documented. (We'll discuss this in more detail in chapter 13, *Know How to Keep Your Books.*)

- Always use the initials "LLC" whenever you use your company name. So on your business cards, stationary, and checks, always have the name of the business followed by "LLC."

- Finally, to let everyone know that you are a member of your LLC, you should always mark correspondence or checks with your name followed by "member" or "manager." These terms indicate that you are acting as on behalf of your LLC and not on your personal behalf.

Taxes

As with sole proprietorships and partnerships, LLCs are pass-through tax entities, meaning that the LLC's taxes are passed through to the members.

For federal tax purposes, the IRS considers LLCs as "disregarded entities"; that is, they are treated as other forms of business and have no separate tax status of their own. Single member LLCs usually choose to handle their taxes exactly the same way as a sole proprietor does. Multiple-member LLCs usually choose to handle their taxes in the same way as a partnership does. Or, an LLC can choose to handle their taxes as a corporation does.

Pros and Cons

Most tax and legal experts really like LLCs, and many recommend that every business owner that is considering becoming a sole proprietor instead become an LLC. There are really no drawbacks to an LLC for most small businesses except the fee to start it. And frankly, if you don't have the money for the fee, you probably can't afford to risk starting a business.

In most states the fee to open your LLC is about $100 and takes only a few minutes. Some states allow you to apply online.

Is an LLC Right for Me?

An LLC may be the best business entity for you if:

- You have personal assets worth protecting.

- You want your business to have legal status and be recognized by the state.

- You want to keep your taxes as simple as possible.

- You want the flexibility to grow your business.

CORPORATIONS

Corporations are the oldest and most complex form of legal entity. For a long time, setting up a corporation was the only way to protect your personal assets from business debt. The complex startup procedure put off many small business owners.

Corporations today come in a variety of types, most notably the traditional C Corp and S Corp. There are other types, but these are the most common.

C Corps

Regular corporations are known as C Corporations and were the only type of corporation until 1958. The discussion below covers corporations in general and C Corps in particular.

Control

The whole premise of a corporation is that it is its own legal entity. For legal purposes, corporations are considered to be their own persons, having their own rights and obligations. It is therefore separate from any employee, shareholder, or executive working for or owning the corporation. Like people, corporations can break the law, they owe taxes, and they can be sued.

One of the advantages of a corporation is that they can sell ownership in the form of stock. Money raised from the sale of stock can then provide the capital to get the corporation off the ground or to finance expansion. But at the same time, selling stock means selling ownership, and if you sell more than 51 percent of the stock, you no longer control the corporation. Many entrepreneurs have started corporations, seen them grow successfully, and then have been summarily ejected from the corporation by their own board of directors. Like children, corporations can take on a life of their own.

Liability

The whole reason corporations were created was to shelter the owners, executives, and employees of a business from the legal liability of running the business. And no form of business entity offers more liability protection than a corporation. It is fairly rare for those owning or working in a corporation to lose anything more than their investment when a corporation gets sued. That doesn't mean that attorneys don't try, it's just that the law looks favorably on this "corporate shield" or "corporate veil" that separates the corporation from those running it, working for it, or owning it.

Adapting to Changes

Because they are legal entities and tend to be larger businesses, corporations can have trouble adapting to a changing market. Some do better than others. You can think about corporations as the battleships of business entities; they can be large and powerful, but take a long time to turn and stop.

Taxes

There is a substantial amount of paperwork involved in establishing and maintaining a corporation, including more complex taxes. Taxes for a simple corporation are usually more complex, and usually more expensive to prepare, than for most sole proprietors or LLCs. Unlike these entities, which pass through their income to the owners, C Corps pay their own income taxes (they are their own "persons," recall). Plus, if the corporation pays dividends to stockholders, that is considered income to the stockholders and they have to pay taxes, too (that's the evil double taxation).

Corporate taxes will almost always have to be handled by a professional, as most solo business owners won't have the expertise or the time to handle these matters on their own.

S Corps

An S Corp is a corporation that has elected to be taxed as a pass-through business entity. Because setting up and running a traditional corporation was so burdensome, in the late 1950s, S Corps were created to give small businesses the liability protection of corporations while making their taxes somewhat simpler. Until LLCs came along in the early 1990s, they were the only good way to get this protection without forming a full-scale C Corp.

S Corps can have one owner, who is an employee of the business, which means he or she is paid a salary. This salary is subject to payroll taxes. But all remaining profits from the business are owned by the business and distributed to the owners, and so is not subject to payroll taxes. If structured properly, S Corp owners with profitable businesses can save substantially on their taxes this way. But in some circumstances, the opposite may be true. See an accountant if you think you could benefit from forming an S Corp.

S Corps have been largely replaced by LLCs, which offer much of the same liability protection and tax simplification without the additional paperwork required of a corporation.

Pros and Cons

In general, corporations lend themselves to businesses that face significant liability, need to generate substantial capital, or have significant income. Most solo business owners who don't fall into these categories just don't want the additional paperwork and costs associated with starting and running a corporation. If you think a corporation is right for you, consult with an accountant or an attorney to see if a corporation makes business and financial sense.

Is a Corporation Right for Me?

A corporation may be the best business entity for you if:

- You have significant personal assets worth protecting.

- Your business faces significant liability, needs to generate substantial capital, or will generate significant income.

- You don't mind sharing control of the business with others.

- You can take on the additional paperwork and tax responsibility.

NAIL IT DOWN!

Here's what you need to do to choose and set up a business entity.

Sole Proprietorships

- ❑ Check with local and state government about requirements to register a sole proprietorship; register if necessary.

- ❑ Obtain and complete any tax registration, zoning approval, and seller's permits.

- ❑ Check with and fulfill any local and state requirements, licenses, and regulations for your type of business.

Partnerships

❑ Check with local and state government about requirements to register a partnership; register if necessary.

❑ Obtain and complete any tax registration, zoning approval, and seller's permits.

❑ Check with and fulfill any local and state requirements, licenses, and regulations for your type of business.

❑ Create an operating agreement with your partners, including such things as:

    ❑ Each partner's contribution to the partnership.

    ❑ Each partner's rights, responsibilities, and voting powers.

    ❑ How profit and loss will be allocated.

    ❑ How the partnership will be managed.

    ❑ Rules for meeting and taking votes.

    ❑ Any buy/sell or other operating agreements.

    ❑ Any events upon which the partnership will dissolve, including how partners can buy and sell their ownership.

LLCs

❑ File articles of organization with state with a unique name and the initials "LLC."

❑ Obtain and complete any tax registration, zoning approval, and seller's permits.

❑ Check with and fulfill any local and state requirements, licenses, and regulations for your type of business.

❑ Create an operating agreement with your partners if you have a multimember LLC.

Corporations

❑ Consult with attorney and accountant about legal and tax implications of forming a corporation.

❑ File articles of incorporation with state with a unique name.

❑ Create bylaws, a written document that lays out in detail how the corporation will govern itself.

❑ Form a board of directors and hold initial meeting.

❑ Obtain and complete any tax registration, zoning approval, and seller's permits.

❑ Issue stock (if appropriate for the type of corporation).

❑ Create an operating agreement with your partners if you have partners in the corporation.

❑ If you want S Corporation status, check with your experts about forming this entity.

SUMMARY CHART

The chart below summarizes the different business entities we've discussed. You should check with your state regulatory board or attorney to ensure that you understand the limitations and responsibilities of the entity you choose.

	Sole Proprietorship	Partnership	Limited Liability Company (LLC)	Corporation
Basic features	Sole proprietor = one owner. May have employees but no other owners, investors, or partners.	Two or more owners. They have a legal contract to contribute to and benefit from a joint business.	Entity that combines features of sole proprietor and corporation. Simple to establish and run without complexity.	A business entity that carries its own legal and tax status. Is distinct from owners, board, or employees.
Ease and cost of formation	**Easy.** Very easy to establish, essentially free (fees and licenses may be required).	**Not hard.** Certificate of Partnership can be filed with state, minimal cost.	**Not hard.** Article of Organization must be filed with state, usually low cost.	**Fairly complex.** Article of Incorporation must be filed with state, plus filing of bylaws and annual reports.
Control	**Complete.** Owner has complete control and gets to keep all of the profits.	**Depends.** What will you do if partners disagree? Written partnership agreement (Buy/Sell) should be used.	**Depends.** Complete if single member. May be more difficult with multiple members.	**May be very low.** Laws and number of owners limits control.

	Sole Proprietorship	Partnership	Limited Liability Company (LLC)	Corporation
Liability	**Complete.** Owner has complete liability for all business debts and actions.	**Significant.** General partners have complete liability; limited partner's liability limited to investment.	**Very low.** Liability limited to original capital investment. Must maintain LLC formalities.	**Very low.** Risk to owners limited to investment except in unusual cases. Must maintain corporate formalities.
Adapting to changes	**Easy.** The owner can do what they want at any time.	**Can be difficult.** What will you do if partners disagree?	**Can be difficult.** May not be hard for single-member LLC; may be more difficult for multiple-member LLC.	**Very difficult.** Because the corporation may have many owners, change can be slow and time consuming.
Taxes	**Easy.** Profit generally calculated on Schedule C and reported as income on owner's 1040 (pass-through).	**Not hard.** Taxes are paid by partners as in SP (pass-through), but partnership also reports to IRS.	**Easy.** Taxes for single-member LLC handled as in SP; multiple-member LLC can handle taxes as partnership.	**Can be complex.** S Corp handled as in partnership. C Corp pays its own taxes (possibility of double taxation).

Chapter Four

KNOW WHO WILL HELP YOU

U nless you are really smart, talented, and have a lot of free time, you probably don't want to take on all of the different jobs that solo business owners have to accomplish. Your time is best spent earning money, which means doing the work. Nevertheless, other business functions, such as bookkeeping, accounting, insurance, and legal issues, have to be taken care of.

Most successful business owners will get help with these issues before they get into trouble. But many solo business owners make the mistake of not seeking help until after they need it, and sometimes not even then. I suggest you line up someone to help you with your books, an attorney, and an insurance agent before you start doing business. Obviously if you need a loan you'll be in contact with a lender. Look at it this way. If you just moved into a new town, when do you want to meet a doctor—when you have time to shop and pick one you really like, or during a life-threatening emergency?

In this chapter we'll look at the four most common experts you'll want to consult: bookkeepers and accountants, insurance agents, attorneys, and lenders. The goal of this chapter is not to make you an expert in any of these fields, but to make you a smart shopper of these professional services. We'll take an especially close look at insurance, while bookkeeping, accounting, and legal issues are covered in-depth in other chapters.

Remember that part of what you expect from an expert is advice. Don't be afraid to ask tough "what if" questions. Pick their brains; that's part of what you are paying for. But keep in mind that these professionals are advisors; they cannot make your business decisions for you. It is up to you to have enough knowledge and experience about your business to take the advice of professionals and apply it wisely.

Bookkeeping and Accounting

Money is the lifeblood of your business. Just as you can't live without a certain level of blood in your body, if your business loses money, you'll eventually go out of business. It's as simple as that.

This means it is essential that you know how much money your business brings in, how much it spends, and where it goes. Bookkeeping is the process for keeping track of your money as it goes into and out of your business on a daily basis. Accounting allows you to stand back and look at your financial situation, getting the big picture. Both are critical to the health of your business.

How good of a handle do you have to have on your money? My suggestion is that solo business owners, during their first year in business, should know how much money they have in their business checking account at all times, to within a few dollars. If you don't know this, you are not paying enough attention to your books. (We'll discuss bookkeeping basics in chapter 13, *Know How to Keep Your Books*.)

Bookkeeping Options
Many business owners want to keep a tight grip on the money that comes through the business, and this is

completely understandable. On the other hand, if you took the time and effort to know as much about bookkeeping as a bookkeeper or accountant, you might as well go into business as one.

Lots of business owners strike a balance between knowing little about keeping the books and being experts. They get some training or have someone teach them the basics, and then let the experts do the rest. It is always a good idea to have some background in bookkeeping and accounting, if only to know how much you can do, and to be able to evaluate the service others are doing for you. You should, for example, have a good understanding of the topics discussed later in this book.

If your bookkeeping needs are too great for you to handle alone, and that would include nearly every beginning business owner, you have several options.

Computerizing Your Books

You might think that putting your finances on a computer will make your life easier. However, for many beginning businesses, trying to computerize your books right away may not be a good idea. You see, computer bookkeeping programs automate many of the steps that you would perform manually if you do your books on paper, making these steps invisible to you. As long as you are familiar with what the computer is doing behind the scenes this isn't a problem. But if you don't have a thorough understanding of accounting procedures before you start using a computer, you will find it confusing. Small mistakes can quickly mushroom into large ones that you can't track down.

Hire a Professional

The other major option is to hire someone who can help you with your accounting problems. You have lots of choices when it comes to getting help, including using several different levels of help with your accounting needs.

Bookkeepers

Bookkeepers are people with the training to help you keep your books; that is, they may take all of your invoices and receipts for the month, write checks for you, balance your checkbook, and create a profit and loss statement for you at the end of each month. Bookkeepers tend to be small business people themselves and work for many clients for a few hours a month each. Bookkeeper fees typically run $25–$50 an hour.

Accountants

If your needs are more sophisticated, you may want to consider an accountant. Accountants have college degrees and generally specialize in the areas of law and taxes rather than in day-to-day bookkeeping. For example, if your tax needs were complicated or you needed advice on employee payroll taxes, an accountant might be the person to see. Accountant fees typically run $50–$100 an hour.

Certified Public Accountants

Finally, if you really need an expert, you'll want to see a Certified Public Accountant (CPA). A CPA is an accountant who has had additional training and taken a rigorous state test to gain the title of CPA. Not surprisingly, CPAs are your most expensive option. Often CPAs work in a firm, although there are also solo CPAs. Small firms charge $75–$125 an hour, while large firms often charge $150 an hour or more.

LEGAL ADVICE

Most of us want to stay away from lawyers, and for good reason. Lawyers, like hospitals, are usually only used when something has gone wrong and things don't look good. But just as you are probably better off seeing a doctor every year or two because she might catch something early, you are probably better off seeing a lawyer before you start your business rather than when you are on life support.

There are many legal issues you have to confront when you start a business. Here are a few:

- Business entity

- Intellectual property

- Independent contractors

- Contracts

We discussed your legal entity in chapter 3; we'll talk about the other issues in chapter 5, *Know Your Rights and Obligations*.

A mistake in any one of these areas could put you out of business. Chances are one or two consultations with an attorney would reduce or eliminate the possibility of that mistake.

Attorney's fees can be all over the map, depending on whether the attorney works solo or in a firm, has an area of specialty or is a generalist, works in a big city or small town, etc. Typical attorney fees where I live run about $100–$200 an hour.

Attorneys, like accountants, usually charge by the hour; in fact, they'll charge by the minute for short visits or phone calls. Most will provide a free initial half or full hour of consultation to get to know you. After that, though, all fees are on the clock.

INSURANCE

Insurance is kind of a strange product, if you think about it. You are paying for a service that you never want to use. It is much better, and you'll be a lot happier in the long run, if you have insurance but never need it. On the other hand, there is no sense having insurance for things that you don't need to insure. In this section we'll look at what insurance is, how to purchase it, and what kinds of insurance you should consider for your business.

The idea behind insurance is pretty simple. A large group of people all contribute to a pool of money, which is managed by an insurance company. When one of those people has a loss that is covered, the insurance company reimburses them from the pool that everyone has paid into. Since you don't know if you'll ever have a loss, the only way to guarantee that you will be covered is to pay into the pool. If you aren't covered, you will be entirely responsible for your own loss.

Regardless of the type of business you run, the business entity you chose, or any other factor, insurance is your first line of defense against losing your business due to accidents.

Buying Insurance

You should shop for insurance the same way you would shop for any other high-end item like a car or house; that is, carefully. You generally purchase business insurance from an insurance agent, a person whose job it is to know about insurance and get you the coverage your business will need. Insurance agents work for two different types of firms.

Types of Agents

The first is an independent agent. Independent agents do not work for any particular insurance company. Instead they represent a variety of companies and can do some "shopping around" for you. It is common for an independent agent to provide you with quotes from several companies. This is usually to your benefit, but because agents work on commission, some less scrupulous agents may recommend the policy that is best for them, rather than the best for you.

The other type of insurance agent is the one that works for just one company, such as American Family or State Farm. For this reason they are called captive or exclusive agents. These agents can only give you a quote for one company, but their quotes may well be competitive with whatever the independent agent can provide.

Remember that when you buy insurance, you not only buy the policy, but also get the services of the agent. You may find an agent who comes with a personal recommendation and who you would work well with, but can't offer you the cheapest policy. You may decide that it is worth the few extra dollars to get the extra service this agent can provide. As with all professionals, it is best to ask around, shop around, and look for recommendations from others in business.

It is a good idea to get at least three estimates before you purchase a business policy. An independent agency can give you more than one quote because they sell for several companies, and it is a good way for you to get a feel for how responsive an agent is. Make sure that the policies you are comparing cover exactly the same things. It is all too easy to compare apples to oranges when shopping for insurance.

Shopping for Insurance

Before you go shopping for insurance, you should have a very good idea of what your business is and what risks it faces. Only you can know these for sure. If you have an unusual business, the insurance company may have a hard time categorizing you, and the better defined your business is the better the insurance company can insure you. You don't want to fall into any of these traps because you don't know your business:

- You do not want to purchase coverage for things that your business will never encounter.

- You do not want to cover the same thing twice.

- But you also don't want to fail to get complete coverage.

Your agent will provide guidance in these areas, but you'll need to know your business well enough to purchase just the right coverage. Be honest with the agent. If you mislead the agent or forget to mention important details, you might find yourself denied coverage on a claim.

Insurance Terms

In addition to knowing what risks your business faces, you should also have a good idea of what kinds of insurance are available. We'll talk now about some insurance terms and then take a look at different types of insurance.

Premium

A premium is the fee that you pay to carry insurance. Premiums are typically paid quarterly, semiannually, or annually, directly to the insurance company by the date due. Some policies may have a grace period after the due date, during which the premium must be paid to keep the policy in effect.

Deductible

When you have insurance and sustain a loss, you will typically not be covered for the first $250 or $500 of the loss. This amount is called the deductible, and the higher your deductible the lower your premium. Deductibles keep the cost of insurance down because small losses are common and expensive to process.

You should ask yourself how much of a loss you can afford without coverage. If you can afford a $500 or even a $1000 deductible, you will save substantially on your premium, and should end up paying less overall in the long run.

Full Replacement

Besides the deductible, you can choose to insure either the entire replacement cost of your loss, or only a certain percentage. When you have full-replacement coverage, you are reimbursed the cost to replace what was covered, in today's dollars, minus the deductible. For example, if you use a cash register and it is destroyed in a burglary, the insurance company will pay you whatever it costs to replace either that same cash register or a comparable new one. Note that if the cost of the item has increased due to inflation, the insurance covers the increased cost as well.

A less expensive option is actual cash value, where the insurance company pays you the actual current value of the items lost, which takes into account depreciation. This means that if the damaged cash register is five years old and has lost 50 percent of its value, you would only get 50 percent of what you paid for it. Actual cash value is cheaper, but most business owners prefer to get full replacement because they don't want to worry about making up any difference in cost.

Rider or Endorsement

When you purchase a policy, it protects many common items. You may have things that are not covered in a standard policy, but are too valuable to be left uncovered. Whenever you add an item to be covered that normally is not, you purchase what is called a rider or an endorsement. This is simply an addition to your regular coverage, and the additional coverage "rides along" with the normal coverage. We'll talk about some common riders later.

Business Owner's Policy

Most small business owners will purchase a package of coverages from an insurance company known as a Business Owner's Policy, or BOP. BOPs include most major coverages a business owner will need, and by purchasing a package you will save money compared to buying the coverages separately. BOPs cover both property and liability, as explained in the next section.

What to Cover

Generally, businesses and individuals need to insure two things: property and liability. You insure against property losses so that in the case of fire, flooding, or other destructive perils, you can replace the business property you lose. Liability coverage protects you in case someone is hurt or something is damaged as the result of you doing business. We'll take a look at each of these in more detail.

Property Insurance

Property insurance covers against the loss of physical assets owned by the business that are damaged or destroyed. For example, if your business burns down, you would want to have your insurance cover the cost of any inventory, machinery, and equipment you had. There are many ways you could sustain such a loss, of course, and there are different types of policies that cover different types of damage. The most basic, and cheapest, type of property insurance coverage you can purchase is called standard form. It only covers you for the perils that are named in the policy. Commonly named perils include fire, hail, and wind. If your loss results from any other cause, you aren't covered. So if you have a standard form policy that doesn't specifically include damage due to a sewer backing up, for example, and the sewer backs up, you are out of luck.

The most complete form of coverage is special form, which covers you against loss regardless of the cause, unless that cause is specifically excluded. Exclusions you'll usually find in all insurance policies include things like war and riot, which are very small risks indeed for most of us. Special form has the advantage in that if your loss comes from an unusual cause, you will be covered. Special form is more expensive than standard form, but it is also more popular because most business owners don't want to worry about having a loss from an uncommon cause. Also, special form is the only type of property coverage that normally covers theft, which is when a stranger steals from you (as opposed to employee theft). With standard form, you would have to purchase that coverage as a rider (an addition) to your regular policy.

You might think that if you work out of your home your homeowner's insurance would cover your business equipment, but this often is not the case. Usually your homeowner's or renter's insurance will not cover business equipment unless you get a rider adding your business equipment to your personal coverage. Usually this rider is not that expensive and could be worth the cost if your business equipment is valuable to you.

Common Riders

So, you decide to purchase special form property coverage and everything your business owns is covered, right? Well, not quite. There are some special items that property insurance does not typically cover because of special risks. To cover these items you will have to purchase a rider to your policy that will cover these items. You have to decide if the risk of loss is worth the cost.

Computer

Computer insurance covers hardware, software, and the cost of the data on the computer. For many businesses, simply backing up your data is a more cost-effective way of insuring against a crashed computer. If your business has a large investment in computer equipment or creates valuable information, computer coverage is worth looking into, because the insurance company will pay not only to replace the computer hardware and software, but also the cost (including labor) of replacing the data on it.

Floater

If your business requires you to physically move equipment from one location to another, it might not be covered because most policies assume that your business stays in one place. If you have, say, portable photography equipment that is damaged away from your business, it may not be covered unless you have a rider for these items, called a floater. Also, if your business involves taking possession of items that belong to someone else, as in a bike-repair business, you should consider coverage for that (called bailee's coverage).

Employee Theft

This is not covered under property insurance policies and is separate from theft insurance. Instead you would purchase a commercial blanket bond, which is a policy that covers a business for theft by its employees for a fixed amount, regardless of the number of employees involved.

Business Interruption

This coverage replaces your income if your business is closed due to unexpected interruptions caused by perils covered in your policy. Note that things like your being ill or construction on the street in front of your business are not covered. The amount the insurance company pays you is determined by your history of income during a comparable period, and the insurance company will work with you to get your business up and running as quickly as possible.

Loss of Rent

Similar to business interruption, this coverage pays your rent if your business loses income due to unexpected interruptions, such as fire.

Key Person

This coverage replaces lost income when a person essential to your business cannot work, and it will pay the salary or fees of someone to replace the key person. Note that key-person coverage only comes into play if the covered person is lost due to death or disability.

Plus, despite how important we think we are, key-person coverage is usually not a cost-effective way to insure ourselves as business owners. Chances are you do not have the unusual skills or knowledge that would make it difficult to replace yourself on the open market. Usually disability or life insurance are better options to protect your income in case you can't work.

Workers' Compensation and Unemployment

Most states require most businesses with employees to carry workers' compensation and unemployment compensation insurance. Because sole proprietors and single-member LLCs owners are not generally considered employees of their business, they are exempt from these requirements on themselves (obviously, their employees, if any, must be covered). However, you should check with your insurance agent to find if your personal insurance will cover you in case of a work-related injury. You may find that workers' compensation is a cheap way of covering yourself in all situations. In most states these coverages are sold through the same insurance agents that sell other business policies.

Liability Insurance

The other major form of insurance is liability insurance. Liability insurance covers three things:

- Bodily injury to others that results from your doing business.

- Property damage that results from your doing business.

- Legal fees resulting from torts.

An example of how liability insurance would cover you as the result of bodily injury would be if you had a retail store and someone slipped and fell while in your store. The insurance company would pay his or her medical bills. In a similar way, liability insurance also protects you if you damage someone's property; for example, if as part of your cleaning service you accidentally damage a client's antique vase.

The third, and often most important thing, liability insurance covers are the legal fees resulting from torts. "Tort" is the name for when someone sues you in court. If your insurance company decides to contest a liability claim, they pay for your attorney and court fees in the dispute.

Just as your personal property insurance probably doesn't cover your business equipment, any personal liability insurance you have probably won't cover you in cases where there is a liability issue with your business. You will have to have separate business liability insurance.

Umbrella Policy

Liability policies are usually purchased in a specific amount that may not be enough if there is an unusual and catastrophically large loss. You can purchase an umbrella policy to protect against these rare occurrences. An umbrella policy offers you extra liability insurance that pays for a loss when the limits of your underlying policy are reached. Umbrella policies are not very expensive considering how much coverage you can get, typically $1 million or more, and doubling your umbrella coverage is not expensive.

How Much Liability Do I Need?

The amount of coverage you need is based on three factors. First, what risks do you face? Some businesses, such as consultants, face little if any risk and so would need little liability insurance. Some other business, such as a retail or trucking business, would probably want a lot of coverage as their risks are much greater.

Second, what can you afford? How much money you have to start may also determine how much coverage you can afford. You can always increase coverage as your business grows.

The final, and best, test is, how well do you want to sleep at night? Can you sleep well knowing that you face a risk that you may not be able to afford?

Auto Insurance

Chances are you own a car in your own name and will use it in your business. However, using your personal car for business purposes may put you in a gray area with your insurance company. Insurance companies may want you to carry more expensive business insurance if they know you are using your car for business. Some insurance experts recommend keeping your personal coverage when starting your business and not telling the insurance company. But if your agent or insurance company asks if you use your car for business, tell the truth. Withholding information from the insurance company is considered fraud and may be grounds for denial of coverage.

If your business becomes large enough and you have your business buy and insure a car, you'll have to let your agent know.

Also, you may be liable for any auto accidents caused by an employee driving on business, whether it is your car or theirs. If you have employees who drive on business, make sure that they have their own adequate auto insurance, and make them prove it to you before you have them drive.

LENDERS

If you need outside funds to help start your business, you may be afraid to approach a bank or other lenders. You think that they are out to trip you up, to simply find reasons not to give you a loan. But bankers and other lenders exist for the purpose of lending you money. That is their product, and getting their loans repaid is how they make their money. The last thing they want to do is repossess your assets and sell them; banks are in the lending business, not the repossession business.

Lenders Profit When You Succeed

Lenders make money when you succeed. They want your business to thrive. But at the same time, they need to reduce their risks; that's why they are so picky about who they lend money to. And that's one reason why lenders like to see good business plans, because anyone who shows the determination, perseverance, and patience to complete a business plan has a much greater chance of business success than someone who doesn't.

We'll discuss what lenders look for in businesses seeking loans in chapter 11, *Know Where the Money Will Come From.*

How Can I Afford This Help?

Although the fees for these professionals may sound like a lot, remember that you generally only need to consult with these folks a few hours a month, or even a year. If your accounting needs are simple, you may find that you can keep your own books but that you need an accountant to help you with taxes at the end of the year. Or perhaps you'll have a bookkeeper maintain your books during the year and prepare your taxes, but then you'll have a CPA look over your tax forms before you submit them.

Plus, you might be able to handle some simple legal matters on your own, but it is almost always a good idea to run your problem and possible solution past an attorney before you go it alone.

How Much Experts Really Cost

One way to look at the cost involved in hiring experts is by thinking about how long it would take you to do what an accountant does. For example, let's say it takes you, the book-keeping novice, six hours to do your end-of-the-quarter books, including generating your financial statements and preparing your quarterly taxes. Your accountant, being the pro, could do this for you in two hours. She might charge you $100 an hour, for a total of $200. Yikes! Sounds like a lot! Until you stop to consider that if you spent your six hours doing billable work instead of slaving over your books, you should be able to earn at least $240, enough to pay the cost of the accountant and put some spare change in your pocket. (Plus, professional fees are tax deductible!)

As for the value of attorneys, remember the old phrase "penny wise and pound foolish." Investing a couple of hundred dollars consulting an attorney over a contract or business deal worth thousands is definitely money well spent, if only for the peace of mind knowing that everything is in order.

Finally, remember that the cost of the insurance agent's advice is free, so use their knowledge to protect your business from the unpredictable.

NAIL IT DOWN!

The first step in nailing down the professional services offered by accountants, attorneys, and insurance agents is to figure out exactly how much money you have to spend on these services. And if you can't afford to at least touch base with the experts and purchase adequate insurance, you should probably take a closer look at how likely it is that your business can succeed.

❑ Develop a budget that will show how much you can spend on annual bookkeeping, accounting, and legal fees based on the complexity of your business.

❑ Come up with a figure for your insurable property assets and a figure for liability coverage based on your knowledge of the industry and the risks your business faces.

Bookkeeping and Accounting

You have a wide variety of options when it comes to getting help with your books. Remember, even if you have the time and expertise, sometimes it is cheaper to hire outside help.

Checklist: Bookkeepers and Accountants

❑ Evaluate your time and expertise in determining what levels of help you need.

❑ Get training, if required, to get up to speed on book-keeping basics.

❑ Seek out recommendations from other business people, chambers of commerce, or professional organizations.

❑ Interview several firms or individuals to find a good match for your specific needs.

Legal Advice

Everyone would probably be happier if they didn't have to use attorneys. But think of your attorney as someone who can help keep you out of trouble and who can provide advice that will allow your business to run more smoothly.

Checklist: Attorneys

❑ Many state bar associations will be happy to refer you to several attorneys working in your area who can help you.

❑ Seek out recommendations from other business people, chambers of commerce, or professional organizations.

❑ Interview several firms or individuals to find a good match for your specific needs.

Insurance

Unlike accountants and attorneys, the services of an insurance agent are free to you, so you shouldn't feel shy about asking for advice. And remember, it is always better to figure out how to avoid a loss in the first place rather than to have great insurance after a loss.

Checklist: Insurance

❑ Know exactly what your business is and what risks you face.

❑ Seek out recommendations from other business people, chambers of commerce, or professional organizations.

❑ Get three quotes on identical policies covering both property and liability.

Chapter Five

KNOW YOUR RIGHTS AND OBLIGATIONS

Businesses face a variety of pitfalls on the way to success. You may not look at it this way, but the law provides you with protections from many of these pitfalls. However, the law protects you only if you agree to play by the rules. Many solo business owners will try to bend the rules to their advantage, but doing so usually backfires. By bending the rules, you put yourself at a disadvantage. You can put yourself at risk from others who seek to take advantage of you, and you make it more difficult on yourself when you decide to go legitimate.

In this chapter we'll look at some of the more common legal issues small businesses face and some common-sense ways to stay out of trouble. The issues we'll look at are:

- Employees vs. independent contractors

- Contracts

- Intellectual property

Before we get into the details, just let me remind you that the information here is not legal advice. Rather, it is information that you should know in helping to understand legal issues and when seeking professional legal assistance.

Employees vs. Independent Contractors

Hiring employees can be a difficult process. You have to do the advertising, recruiting, interviewing, training, payroll, and, in many cases, firing of the worker. Many small business owners try to avoid having these headaches if they can.

There are a couple of ways around hiring employees. One is to contact a temporary employment agency. You don't have to interview, hire, fire, or pay the employee; you just negotiate a price with the temp service and pay them. They handle the rest. You can expect to pay about twice what you would pay an employee per hour, but many businesses, large and small, think it is worth the cost if the job is not a permanent one. It is at least worth a phone call.

Another option is to hire independent contractors. An independent contractor (IC) is a business person that you hire not as an employee but as a business. They work for you on a contract basis, and you pay them a negotiated fee. Unlike an employee, you do not have to calculate and withhold payroll taxes from an IC; he or she is responsible for his or her own income and self-employment taxes. Sounds pretty nice so far, right? Let's look at the legal distinctions between employees and independent contractors and find out why the IRS takes such an interest in the difference.

Employees
When you work for someone else, you are an employee and the hiring party is an employer. As an employer, they tell you what work to do, when, and where to do it. They provide

you with the tools, and often the training, to complete your work. Employees generally perform the same tasks day after day, indefinitely. In return the employer provides you with a regular salary, but from that paycheck they withhold your income, Social Security, and Medicare taxes.

In other words, when you are an employee, the employer is in control of what you do, and they withhold your taxes. At the end of the year, the employer provides its employees with a W-2 showing their income and taxes withheld.

Independent Contractors

When you are self-employed, you are considered an independent contractor when you do a job for someone else, either a business or an individual. Generally, ICs are hired to complete a specific assignment or job. ICs generally work on a job according to their schedule and with their own tools.

The check an IC receives is just for the work—no tax is withheld, because the IC is not an employee. But since the government still expects to get its share of taxes, the IC is responsible for paying his or her own taxes, both income taxes and self-employment taxes, which includes both Social Security and Medicare. (We'll talk more about how self-employment taxes work in chapter 15, *Know How to Minimize Your Taxes*.)

In other words, when you are an independent contractor, you are in control of what you do, and you are responsible for paying your own taxes. At the end of the year, anyone paying an IC more than $600 must provide them and the IRS a Form 1099, showing the total amount paid.

When you are an employee	When you are an IC
Employer withholds income, SS, and other taxes from wages	You are responsible for paying all income and self-employment taxes (estimated taxes)
Employer provides W-2 showing wages paid and taxes withheld	Business may be required to provide you and IRS with Form 1099 to report what it paid you

Why the Government Cares

It probably comes as no surprise that some folks will try to use the independent contractor role to avoid paying taxes. By calling an employee an IC, the hiring party thinks they can avoid paying payroll taxes and unemployment compensation. Workers can claim that they thought they were an employee, and so they thought they didn't have to pay taxes. Whether either party fails to make the proper tax payments intentionally or through ignorance, the law is clear: Workers are either employees or independent contractors, and the proper taxes must be paid.

Why You Should Care

But it just isn't cheaters who can get into trouble when they deliberately fail to pay the proper taxes. You can too, if you accidentally categorize a worker for tax purposes. Let's say that you hire a bookkeeper part time to help you with your business. If the two of you aren't clear on whether your relationship is that of employer and employee or hiring party and independent contractor and no one pays the taxes, someone is going to get in trouble. It could be you.

A similar situation may exist for workers' compensation insurance. Generally employers must purchase workers' comp for their employees, but businesses hiring ICs do not. Let's say you hire a worker and treat him or her as an IC, when the law would consider him or her an employee. If that worker gets hurt on the job and then gets medical treatment, he or she will be asked if the injury is the result of work. When he or she says yes, that will trigger your state's workers' comp system, and you, as the hiring party, could be looking at penalties as well as paying the worker's medical bills.

Staying Out of Trouble

The easiest thing to do to avoid getting into trouble is to make sure the independent contractor, either yourself or the one you are doing business with, is an LLC. With a sole proprietor, there can always be a question as to whether the proprietor is a "real business" or simply a very short-term employee. If your business is an LLC, there isn't any question that it is a real business (the same would go for a corporation).

If you are a sole proprietor, be sure and get an EIN from the IRS (see chapter 15 for details), and be sure to register to pay all required income and sales taxes with your state. These actions help establish the business as legitimate. If you are hiring a sole proprietor, ask for his or her EIN and be sure to remind him or her that you will file a form 1099 with the IRS.

The chart below poses some of the questions that federal or state taxing authorities will ask to determine if the proper classification for a worker is an employee or an independent contractor. If it isn't clear to you that a worker is one or the other (and there can easily be situations where it isn't clear), contact the IRS and your state. For federal tax purposes, you can order IRS Form SS-8. This form has a series of questions that you can answer and send to the IRS. They'll let you know if they consider the position an employee or IC.

You should also check with your state. Some states have rules that are stricter than the IRS, and they may actually provide rulings that contradict the IRS (another good reason to get that LLC).

If the question is...	An employee would answer	IC would answer
Who determines where, when, and how the work is done?	My employer	Me
Who sets the working hours?	My employer	Me
Does the worker have to work on-site?	Yes	No
Who pays the worker's expenses?	My employer	Me
Who furnishes the tools or materials?	My employer	Me
Does the worker work for more than one business?	No	Yes
Does the worker maintain a separate place of business?	No	Yes

Questions the IRS and your state may ask to determine if a worker is an independent contractor or employee

CONTRACTS

Nobody likes dealing with contracts. You want to do business with someone and they shove this long document in front of you with terms you don't understand and they expect you to sign it. Isn't a handshake enough?

Although I would encourage you to do business only with those for whom a handshake is enough, I would also strongly discourage you from not backing up that handshake with a written contract. Contracts don't need to be long, hard-to-read documents that no one understands. Actually, contracts can be simple documents, and they can save your business.

Think of it this way. How far would a football game get if the players had to argue about the rules every time someone did something questionable? Instead, the game has written rules that state how the game will be played and referees to enforce the rules. The law provides your business with some general rules, and you can use contracts to specify exactly what the rules of your game will be.

Contracts Solve Problems Before They Begin

The power of contracts is not that they give you the ability to prove your side is right if you have to go to court (although they may let you do this). Their power comes from the fact that, because the parties to the contract have already discussed the issues between them, disputes are much less likely to arise. Everyone goes into the contract knowing what should happen, so there are no surprises. And if there is a dispute, the contract should state clearly how it should be resolved.

What Makes a Contract Valid

The concept of a contract is pretty simple. Contracts are simply legally enforceable agreements between parties in exchange for something of value. Let's break this down and look at it word by word.

Legally enforceable agreement . . .

This means that the contract can be used to enforce an agreement, that either party can seek legal remedies by taking it into court to back up what was agreed to.

. . . between parties . . .

This means that all of the parties involved must agree to the contract. In other words, the contract is assumed to be voluntary; no one can force you into a contract.

. . . in exchange for something of value.

To be valid, the contracting parties must agree to exchange things of value. Usually this means money in exchange for goods or services, but it can mean anything of value. If I offer you a bite of my sandwich in return for some of your potato chips, technically we have a contract because we have agreed to exchange items of value. On the other hand, if I just asked for a potato chip and you said OK, there is no contract because I didn't offer anything in return.

This idea of offer and acceptance is essential for a valid contract. For each contract, one side must make an offer, and the other side must either accept or reject it. If you are offered a contract and don't like something about it, you are free to make changes and then use these as the basis for a counteroffer. The other side then gets the chance to do the same. Once an offer is accepted, perhaps after a period of negotiation, the contract takes effect.

Special Contracts

Standard Contracts

Sometimes you'll be asked to sign a contract and told you don't need to read it or that you can't make changes because "this is a standard contract." There is no such thing as a standard contract. There are contracts that are preprinted, there are contracts that may contain common elements, but there are no standard contracts. Remember, if you sign a contract it means that you are saying you agree with all of its provisions and obligations. That means you had better understand and really agree with those provisions.

You should always show an important or complex business contract to your attorney before signing it. Sometimes contracts have things that are not in your interest, things that attorneys can see more easily than you. Never be rushed into signing a contract.

What if you don't like something in the contract? You can negotiate to make a change before signing it. You can make the change in the contract yourself before signing it, and then the other party can either accept or reject your change. Or you can reject the contract.

Leases

One of the more common contracts many business owners will sign is a lease. If your business has to occupy space your only real options are buying or renting, and since buying is both permanent and expensive, most businesses will sign a lease.

There are two things to remember about leases. The first is that they are like any other contract and can be negotiated. Chances are good the landlord will tell you that this is a standard lease and you don't have to read it. Not only should you read it, you should have your attorney read it as well. Leases often contain clauses that may not be in your interest, and may even be illegal.

Second, don't forget that when you sign a lease, you are agreeing to pay the full value of the lease. For example, if your lease is for $1,000 a month for three years, you are obligated to pay not one month's or even a year's rent, but the full $36,000 value of the lease. If your business folds after six months, you are still on the line for the remaining thirty months.

Verbal vs. Written Contracts

Contracts can take two forms, written or verbal. You might have heard the old saying about the value of a verbal contract: Verbal contracts aren't worth the paper they're written on.

The reason verbal contracts are nearly worthless isn't that they aren't valid (they may be perfectly legal), it's that they are nearly impossible to enforce. If there is a dispute and there is only a verbal contract, how can anyone decide who is really right?

With a written contract, there can be no question about what was agreed to because it is down on paper for all to see. That doesn't mean that contracts have to be complex. The best contracts are those that spell out the offer and acceptance in everyday language that everyone can understand.

Keep It Simple

Contracts should make your business life simpler, not more difficult. Contracts do not have to be complex and full of legal jargon. As long as the contract you draft has the necessary ingredients—an offer and an acceptance for something of value—it is probably valid.

Anyone can write a contract. If you need some help creating contracts, see if your local library has a book with example contracts. An industry association might also have example contracts you could use, or see your attorney for help in writing a contract. And always run a contract past your attorney if the contract is for more than a small amount. You might be able to afford to take a loss on an invalid or unfavorable $100 contract. But if you make a mistake on a contract that ends up costing you $10,000 because you wanted to save $200 on legal fees, you will never quit kicking yourself.

Intellectual Property

If your business is involved in developing new things or creating original works, the law provides you with several important ways of protecting it. These works, called intellectual property, include items such as works of art, new and useful devices, and the ways you identify the items you sell. Intellectual property laws let you profit from your work by giving you the tools to protect its value. We'll look at the three types of intellectual property protection and then ask whether or not these protections can actually benefit you.

Copyright

Whenever you create something such as a painting, sculpture, article or book, movie, or any other intellectual work in a fixed format, copyright law immediately and automatically protects it. This means that the work you create is yours, and you can sell it or modify it in any way you see fit. Others cannot sell it or modify it without your permission. Copyright protection is automatic and lasts for the author's lifetime, plus seventy-five years.

Protecting Your Copyright

Although copyright protection attaches immediately and automatically upon the creation a protected work, there are two things you can do to make your copyright protection stronger. The first is to always put a notice on your work that you understand that the work is yours. You can do this by attaching a copyright notice to the work which includes the word "copyright" along with the creator's name, the date, and usually, the copyright symbol "©." See the copyright at the front of this book for an example.

The second thing you can do is to register your work with the Library of Congress. This step is completely optional, as the law protects your work even if it not registered. But if your work is registered and you decide to seek remedies from an infringer, you may have an easier time proving your claim and may be able to recover greater damages, than if it is not.

Registering your work is easy and not expensive. Most works can be registered online (http://www.copyright.gov)

using the Electronic Copyright Office (eCO) tool. You can either upload your work electronically, or if this isn't practical, the system will print a mailing label for you to physically mail your work to the Copyright Office. Of course, you can also apply for your copyright by mail, but this option costs more and provides no advantages.

Who Needs Copyright

Among solo business owners, copyright protection is most important for authors, artists, and especially musicians. Any work of art can be easily duplicated and sold, and music is something that has the potential to be easily ripped-off and sold. You should consider registering any work you think could be potentially valuable, whether now or in the future.

Trademarks

A trademark is an identifying element for a product or service. For example, if you have a well-known product nearby, such as a can of soda, take a look at its label for a little ™ or ® symbol. These symbols indicate that the creator of the product is using the marked words, symbols, or designs as identifications for the product and is indicating their ownership of them.

Trademark, in other words, puts the world on notice that these elements cannot be used by others to identify similar products.

For example the word "Coke" is a well-known trademark, as is the wavy line found on Coke cans. The ® symbol on the can alerts the world that the Coca-Cola company has registered these elements as identifying their product and that no one else can use them.

Levels of Trademark Protection

There are two levels of trademark protection. The first level is when you believe you are the first to use a mark in identifying a product, and you want to claim that mark as yours. You can immediately, and without cost, put the ™ symbol next to the identifying element as notice that this mark is yours.

The second level is to register your mark with the Patent and Trademark Office (http://www.uspto.gov). Trademark registration is moderately expensive (about $350) and gives you an easier time proving the mark is yours and seeking damages from infringers. Once registered, you can mark your trademark with the registered symbol ®.

Infringement Is a Two-Way Street

Many solo business owners think obtaining trademarks is a great idea, although later I'll give you a reason not to bother. For now, just let me warn you that many more solo business owners will be on the offending end of copyright or trademark law rather than the enforcing end. I've seen many, many examples of businesses violating copyrights and especially trademarks, sometimes without knowing it. It is actually pretty common, especially with things like birthday cakes or perhaps clothing sold at art shows or swap meets. These items may include images or slogans that everyone is familiar with, such as Mickey Mouse or Old Navy. But the businesses selling these items did not have permission to use these elements and are almost certainly violating the law.

(Note that if you use a trademark or copyrighted image for personal use there shouldn't be a problem. For example, if you put a professional sports team's logo on one sweatshirt that you wear, that shouldn't get you in trouble. If you make a batch of these shirts and sell them, that's clearly a violation of the law.)

Don't think that just because you are a small business that you are immune to penalties if you violate these laws. Large corporations are often zealous in their enforcement of their intellectual property and frequently threaten to sue even the smallest of businesses over seemingly minor violations.

You are most likely to violate trademarks when thinking up a business name, but even here it mainly depends on the geographic area where you do business. If you run a small business in one city, and there are no other businesses operating in your area with the same name or same product names, there is usually nothing to worry about.

Businesses often run into trouble when they have the same name as a national firm or when they expand across state lines. What to do? Simple. Find a new name that no one else has.

Discovering whether or not you might be violating someone else's trademark is usually pretty simple. For small geographic regions, begin by checking the phone book. Each state will maintain a list of corporation and LLC names, so if you form one of these entities you can be sure your name is unique in that state. Be sure to check the web for any businesses possibly using the same name as yours and see if theirs is trademarked. Finally, you can check for registered trademarks at the Trademark Office website.

Patents

Patents protect original and useful machines or processes for twenty years. During that time you have complete control of how your patented item is manufactured and sold.

Obtaining a patent is a long, expensive process and usually requires an attorney that specializes in patent law. It is uncommon for a solo business to obtain a patent, although if you have a great idea, it is worth looking into. Most patents will end up costing thousands of dollars to obtain. You can find more information at http://www.uspto.gov.

Some businesses advertise that they can help you decide whether a patent is justified, for a fee. Usually these firms will tell you that your idea is great and then offer to help you get a patent, for an inflated fee. You would be better off having your idea evaluated by an independent organization. Some universities around the country offer this service.

SHOULD YOU PROTECT YOUR WORK?

Not everyone who could potentially use these intellectual property laws should bother using them. Why not?

Cost

First, there is the cost of obtaining protection. As I've mentioned, copyright and trademark protection can be free. Many experts would encourage you to put a copyright notice on any creative works you produce, and there is no harm putting the ™ next to items you think you can trademark. But registering these works, especially trademarks, can get expensive, and I've already mentioned that patents are very costly.

Enforcement

Second, intellectual property laws are only enforceable in one way—when you sue someone you think is violating your rights in court. You can't call the police and expect them to do anything; it is all up to you. That means that if you really want to back up your rights, you have to be willing to go to court, and that will cost several tens of thousands of dollars at a minimum.

So you have to ask yourself, what is the value of my ideas compared to how much I would spend to protect them? Sure, it doesn't cost you anything to trademark a logo for your business, but are you going to bother to register it, much less enforce that trademark in court, if someone else uses it? I don't want to discourage you from protecting your work; your work is valuable and you should take whatever steps you think are necessary to defend it. But be aware that the protection you seek may come at a substantial cost.

For More Information

The government has some excellent information at their websites on intellectual property issues, including search engines that will let you search for trademarks or patents.

Nolo (http://www.nolo.com) can provide you with a lot of information regarding intellectual-property issues. Their website is a great place for basic legal information of all types.

To obtain information on . . .	Contact
Copyright	U.S. Copyright Office: http://www.copyright.gov
Patents and trademarks	U.S. Patent and Trademark Office: http://www.uspto.gov
All of the legal issues mentioned in this chapter	Nolo http://www.nolo.com

NAIL IT DOWN!

Here are some things you can do to stay out of legal trouble.

Employee vs. Independent Contractor

If you aren't sure the correct status for a worker, or for yourself, follow these steps.

❑ Read IRS Publication 1779, Independent Contractor or Employee.

❑ Check with your attorney and accountant.

❑ For federal tax purposes, fill out IRS Form SS-8.

❑ For state tax purposes, check with your state taxing authority.

Contracts

❏ Always use a written contract for any transaction worth more than a trivial sum.

❏ Always consult with your attorney before drafting a contract or signing a contract.

Intellectual Property

❏ For intellectual works in a fixed format such as books, movies, music, or art, it is a good idea to put a copyright notice on the work even though it is protected upon creation.

❏ Before you name your business or a product, verify whether or not the name is already in use by someone else.

❏ If you have a new and useful machine or process, consider a patent if you can afford the expense.

❏ Regardless of the type of intellectual property protection you acquire, it is your obligation to enforce your rights if you want to maintain them.

Chapter Six

KNOW YOUR CUSTOMERS

Why should you care who your customers are? Because without customers you have no business. It is as simple as that. Your customers, also known as your market, will be those people who are willing to buy from you, but not everyone in the world, in the country, or even in your neighborhood, are potential customers. We all have separate tastes and desires, and it is essential that you find who is most likely to buy from you before you start your business. You don't have the time or the money to try and convince people who aren't in your market to buy from you. It's much easier to identify who is most likely to want your product, and then target your marketing to them.

This is what market research is all about; learning who your customers are, what they want, and how you can meet their needs. There are three general steps to doing market research. The first is to become acquainted with the industry, the larger universe in which your business will exist. The second is to know the characteristics of those who comprise your market, your potential customers. And finally, you should know your competition. Knowing your competition is so important that I have given it a separate chapter right after this one.

KNOW YOUR INDUSTRY

Before your customers will spend their cash, they need a motivation. Think about why you purchase something. Your money is hard earned, so you don't want to spend it frivolously. On the other hand, you may buy a lot of things you don't really need. Why? Every person has needs, wants and desires, or problems that they would like to solve. Sometimes these desires and problems can be satisfied or fixed by purchasing something.

Most people buy what they absolutely need, such as food, clothing, and shelter, without too much thought. You have to have these things, no question. But what about other things, like televisions and automobiles and fancy running shoes? Do you need those? No, but many people want them. In fact, you have to want what you buy more than the money it costs to buy them or you wouldn't buy them at all. So for everything you buy there is a desire to be fulfilled or a problem to be solved.

Ask yourself what problem your customer hopes to solve, or what desire they want to fulfill, by purchasing your product. For example, if you sell bagels, there may be several problems or desires your customers may want to take care of. For example, they may be hungry and need to eat. On the other hand, they may just want to have a tasty snack and figure that a bagel is better for them than a pastry (which means that health may be another desire of theirs).

Your customers will always have a desire they want fulfilled, or a problem that they want to solve, and will usually have their choice of ways to fulfill that desire or solve that problem. When someone is offering a product that solves the same problem, in the same way, in the same area, and to the same customers as your product, they are your direct competitors. When someone is using a different way to solve the same problem, they are indirect competitors.

The diagram below shows how a bagel shop's competition is related to it. Many small food establishments would compete directly for customers seeking a quick snack, such as pastry shops or sandwich shops. But potentially, any business that sells food would be an indirect competitor, such as a fast-food restaurant or even the grocery store. We'll discuss how you stack up against your competition in more detail later.

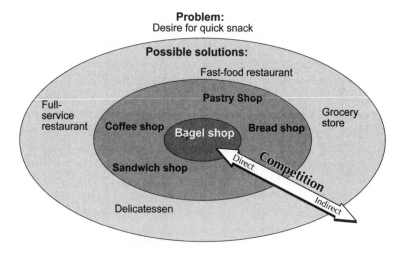

Your industry is made up of all of the businesses that compete for the same customer dollar as you

You will have to know what industry your business is in so that you can compete effectively. By knowing what is happening within the industry, you will be in a better position to compete and to decide how to take advantage of your own strengths and weaknesses.

How Do I Know What Industry I'm In?
There are several ways to figure out what industry you are in. The best way is to have some working experience within

the industry. For example, if you have already worked in a business similar to the one you plan on starting, you are probably aware of the major players, industry associations, and trends within the industry. If not, you will have to do a little more digging.

Another way is to check out NAICS Codes. NAICS stands for North American Industry Classification System, which is a common numbering system used to track business types and industries (it has replaced the older SIC codes, which did the same thing). Each NAICS code can be broken down to identify different industries and sectors, kind of like each house's address can be broken down by state, city, street, and number. Looking at the NAICS code for your business can tell you what industries you are in. For example, let's say a bagel-shop owner named Betsy looks up "bagels" in the NAICS listings for food service businesses. She'll find a listing like this:

NAICS Category	Description	
722	Food Services and Drinking Place	*Industry*
7221	Full-Service Restaurant	Indirect
72211	Full-Service Restaurants	
722110	Full-Service Restaurants	
7222	Limited-Service Eating Places	
72221	Limited-Service Eating Places	
722211	Limited-Service Restaurants	
722212	Cafeterias	
722213	Snack and Nonalcoholic Beverage Bars	Direct

Betsy finds that code number 722213 is probably the best match for her business, because hers is a limited-service eating place. Note that this places her in the food service industry, and suggests that she is competing against snack bars, cafeterias, and other limited service restaurants.

If you would like to look up the NAICS information on your business, here are some resources:

- http://www.naics.com
  Has a good explanation of the codes, plus a search engine that lets you identify possible matches based on your business's keywords.

- http://www.census.gov/eos/www/naics/
  Has a list of resources for more information, including a link to the latest NAICS codes, and a search engine.

- *The North American Industry Classification System Desk Reference*. A book that has all of the codes listed and is available in larger community or business libraries.

Identifying Trends in Your Industry

The world does not stand still, and many businesses that were thriving 100, fifty, or even ten years ago are now mainly memories. For example, 100 years ago blacksmiths thrived because horses needed horseshoes. In the 1980s there were dozens of home-computer companies; today there are a handful. To help ensure your success, you should have a good handle on what is happening in the world that could affect your industry, and thus your business, in the years to come.

For example, there may be technological changes occurring in your industry that could help or hinder your business. Certainly any high-tech business has to understand that what is cutting edge today could be obsolete in the near future.

Service businesses might be more immune to changes in technology, but they are still subject to changes in the economy, demographics, or tastes. As the baby boomers move into retirement, for example, markets will open and close around their needs.

I can't look into the future for you. The future success of your business relies on your being aware of what is going on around you.

Knowing Your Industry

Industries can be large or small, and markets (that is, the number of potential customers) can be large or small. Large players tend go after large markets, so because everybody has to eat, there is a very large market for all types of food. And because many of us need to eat on the run (there's that problem to solve again), many large players have emerged in the fast-food industry. But there are also many small, family-owned restaurants, so there are both large and small players in the food industry.

Generally smaller markets attract smaller players, so anything requiring customization tends to have many smaller competitors rather than a few big ones. But if the market is large enough or wealthy enough, the big boys will want to get involved, as in high-end automobiles, jewelry, or sailboats.

Most solo businesses do best in the small-market, small-player end of the spectrum, although there are exceptions. You need to be aware of how things might change. For example, right now the market for personal chefs is relatively small, and although there is a trade association for personal chefs, there are no national chains or franchises that I am aware of. But this could change tomorrow. If you were interested in becoming a personal chef, you might want to know, for example, if the personal chef industry was growing or shrinking, and the reasons why. You might want to investigate if there were any franchises available or if most were run as solo businesses. You might want to see how large the market currently is and think about some changes that might make it larger, or smaller, in the future.

Some good ways to stay on top of these issues it to become familiar with industry publications, attend relevant trade shows and meetings, join an industry association, and keep up with what is happening in the world.

Get in Touch with Your Industry Associations

One of the great, overlooked resources available to solo businesses is their trade association. There are tens of thousands of associations in the United States. It would be a huge mistake of you not to take advantage of this resource. Many trade organizations offer information on the trends in the industry, demographic and market information, and ways in which you can overcome common problems. Often these organizations have magazines and online resources available to you, and some will have local chapters where you can meet with others in the same business.

Usually these associations will charge you about $100—$200 per year to join, but most who do join feel that it is well worth the investment. If you aren't sure if the organization is right for you, you should contact them and see if they will send you a free copy of their magazine and any other free information they might have.

These groups usually don't advertise themselves outside of the industry, so the best way to become aware of them is to work within the industry before you start your business. If you don't have that luxury, your best bet is a large book entitled *Encyclopedia of Associations*, published by the Gale Research Co. This book lists thousands of organizations all over the world including 23,000 U.S. associations. You can find it at larger public or business libraries.

Searching the World Wide Web if you have Internet access is another option, although it can be hard to find smaller associations this way unless you already know their name. Sometimes just entering the type of business and the word "association" in a search engine will get you where you want to go. You can also try these listings to get started:

- http://www.asaecenter.org

  Provides a searchable list for thousands of associations. On the toolbar, point to Community, then click Directories & Guides, then click Gateway to Associations.

- http://www.ipl.org

  Browse for information on this page, or use the search box on the main screen.

WHO ARE YOUR CUSTOMERS?

What do you need to start a successful business? First, you need something to sell. Second, you need someone to buy it from you, a market. Without a market, there are no customers, no one to buy from you, and without customers there is no business (unless you get pleasure from giving your product or service away!).

A market is simply a population of people who could be your customers. This doesn't mean they will be your customers, only that they could be. Lots of people starting solo businesses say to themselves, "Everyone needs my product," but if that's true, why aren't they using it now? Simple: They don't need it. Your product might very well help lots of people, it might be a great value, but convincing your potential customers of that will be more challenging than you realize.

You do not want to rely on your intuition with this; you need to be able to prove that your market is out there and willing to buy from you. Actually conducting this research is one of the hardest tasks new businesses face, but it can be done.

Will everyone need your product? No. Isn't it more likely that some people will be more inclined than others to buy from you? Of course! Different people live in different areas, have different interests, different tastes, and different amounts of money that may make them more or less likely to want your product. Knowing your potential customer's characteristics allows you to do two things: First, you can more easily target whom you should aim your marketing efforts at. Second, knowing your customers will help you make more sales because you won't waste your time on those less likely to buy from you.

For most solo businesses, the number of customers will be relatively small compared to the total number of people living in your market area. And the total number of your repeat customers will be even smaller. The general rule of thumb is that 80 percent of your business will come from 20 percent of your customers. In other words, the vast majority of your business will come from a very small number of people. This rule, called the Pareto Principle, is a general rule of thumb for many things in life. So, it is in your best interest to identify and target that small number of people to be successful.

Define Your Market

How do you determine just who those people are? You need to look at and define what characteristics your best customers have in common. There are three general ways you can define your customers.

Demographics

One of the ways you can define your market is to look at who is most likely to buy from you. Are your customers likely to be young or old, rich or poor, white or of color? Characteristics such as these define the demographics of your market.

For example, chances are that the income of a person who buys a Hyundai automobile will be less than the income for a typical BMW customer. Every business has to find a niche and then find the customers whose demographics match that niche. In general, any objective characteristic is a demographic trait. Think of it this way—if you can check it off in a box, it's probably a demographic characteristic. For example, is your income this much or this much? What is your education level, and so on.

I'll have some suggestions on finding demographic information later in the chapter.

Geographics

Geography is another important element defining your market. Some businesses are tied tightly to geography. Retail locations can't move, and so their customers must come to them. If there are not enough customers in the market within a certain distance to the store, the business will lose money. Some other businesses take steps to expand their geographic area, by offering a mobile service, for example, so that they can serve their market over a larger area. And businesses selling over the Internet are not restricted by geography at all.

Psychographics

Other factors to consider include your market's lifestyle, self-concept, and behavior. Do your customers prefer brand names, even though these are more expensive? Are they extremely cost conscious? Do they have a lot of free time, or are they always on the go? What is more important to them, time or money?

Knowing what your market cares about, feels, and how they live is as important as knowing where they live. The fancy term to describe these qualities is psychographics. For many consumers, how they view themselves is more important to predicting what they will purchase than their demographics. The more you can learn about your customers, the more you can see what makes them tick, the better you can fulfill their needs, wants, and desires.

Unlike demographic information, which the government collects and freely provides, psychographic information is more specialized and is generally only available from firms that collect it and sell it.

However, you shouldn't let this stop you from developing your own psychographic profile for your customers. Look at your target customers and ask some of these questions:

- What kind of cars do they drive? Or do they use other forms of transportation?

- What are their hobbies, or what do they do on the weekend?

- What kinds of sports do they like?

- What magazines, if any, do they read?

- Do they belong to any organizations?

Chances are that by combining what you can discover about your target market with some freely available demographic information, you can come up with an excellent profile that will help you zero in on where you can find similar customers.

For a chance to see example psychographic profiles for your zip code from companies that sell this information, check out these websites:

- http://www.esri.com/data/esri_data/tapestry.html

- http://www.claritas.com/MyBestSegments/Default.jsp
  (look for the zip-code look-up button)

Find Your Market

How can you discover who your market is before you go into business? Here are three suggestions. First, just ask! Chances are you know some people who might be in the market for your product or service. Ask them what they think about it. How much would they be willing to pay for it? Do they use anything like it now? How far out of their way would they be willing to go to buy it? You can make this type of market research as simple as talking to friends or as complex as carrying out a written survey. In either case you'll want to note what kind of responses you get and look for patterns in the people you talk to.

Second, after you identify your competition, you can see who their market is (we'll talk all about getting to know your competition in the next chapter). Chances are that your market will be closely related, although perhaps not identical, to your competition's.

Third, this is another area where experience in the industry can be invaluable. If you have worked in a business similar to the one you are starting, you already have a good idea of who your customers will be. And you will also be familiar with the trade associations and organizations that can be an excellent source of market information for your industry.

WHAT DO YOUR CUSTOMERS WANT?

Features vs. Benefits

200 Horsepower! 150 Watts! Now with even more active ingredients! Nationally Certified! Preferred by 4 out of 5 doctors! New and improved! Less filling! Tastes great!

We've all been bombarded with claims like these, claims that make the product advertised sound better than the rest. But what is actually being said here?

One of the main ways businesses try to convince you to buy their products is by telling you about the product's features. A feature is a characteristic, trait, or attribute of the product. It is part of what the product is. Features are often used to convince you that the product is better than others because it has something, or more of something, than the competition, or just because it sounds impressive.

Many solo businesses think that they can get by just by telling customers about their features. Perhaps you have more experience than your competition, or your product is made of a different material, or you are in a different location.

Earlier we said that customers usually buy things that would fulfill needs or wants, or else to solve a problem that they believed they had. In other words, customers want the benefits your product provides, and unfortunately, benefits and features are not the same thing. Instead, they are usually opposite sides of the same coin, sides that your customer might not be able to see at the same time.

Here are some examples of features and benefits. Which do you think is more important in motivating customers for each product to buy?

Feature	Benefit
150 Horsepower	Lets you accelerate and pass safely
1.24 Gigahertz	Saves time by solving spreadsheets fast
Super-Duper-Size	You can eat until you're stuffed
Finest Grade Leather	Feels really good when you sit down
1.65 Carat	Bigger than your friend's diamond
New Package, Same Product	None (this is a real example!)

Any time you see numbers associated with a product, it's a feature. Companies broadcast features because they are easy to create and can sound impressive. If you make a product, you are intimately familiar with it, so you know its features. It is harder to decide what the benefits are. And yet, if you just advertise features, you are asking your customers to translate those features into the benefits they really want.

Benefits = Solutions

In most markets, customers really don't care about features. They want benefits. They want the product to fulfill their need, want, or desire, or to solve their problem. Note that benefits, unlike the more objective features, tend to be subjective, personal, and often emotional. For instance, in the example above of Finest Grade Leather, how many would know if this means anything or is just hype? On the other hand, just about everyone knows and can appreciate the feel of soft leather.

And with the diamond (1.65 carat), what usually drives customers isn't the number of carats so much as what the number represents—the status that a large diamond brings. This is an emotional benefit, and such feelings can be very powerful motivators for people. This is why you can use prestige to set your product apart, because many more customers are motivated by prestige than by features.

There are only a few markets where features are of paramount importance. Young markets, where the features change quickly, often have feature-driven customers. In most mature markets, the features of different products are essentially the same, so benefits must be emphasized. For example, the computer industry has gone from feature-driven to mostly benefit-driven over the past several years.

So, when you are going to market your product, should you tell your potential customers only about features? No, don't make them do the extra work of translating from your features to their benefits in their head. Do the translation for them! Think about why customers might want your product, such as how it will fulfill their needs and desires or solve their problems. Provide them with these benefits along with the features of what you sell.

Is There Enough of a Market for Your Business?

Once you have a good idea of what characteristics your customers will have, you can estimate the number of people with these characteristics in your market area. If there are enough of your target customers in your area to support your business, chances of your business success are good.

But be careful! It can be easy to overestimate how large your market really is. What could your business do if you discover that the market isn't large enough for your business? Here are several options:

First, start another type of business. If there isn't enough demand for what you sell, perhaps you would be more successful selling something else.

Second, keep your business idea, but do it somewhere else. If you have a retail location, you might have to move to a different part of town. Or perhaps your town simply isn't big enough, and you would have to move to another city altogether.

Third, you could find a different means of distributing your product. Perhaps a failing bagel shop should explore wholesaling bagels instead of selling them retail. Perhaps your product would work better being sold via mail order, or over the Internet. We'll look briefly at some of the ways you can distinguish your product later.

Discovering More about Your Market

Market research can often be time consuming and frustrating. It is not an exact science, and finding specific information can be difficult. But it is better than guessing. Many businesses discover too late that the market is smaller than they anticipated.

The first step, as I discussed earlier, is to identify who you think your market is. Next, it would be nice if you could put some numbers on how many people fit these categories in your business area.

A good way to do this is by looking at census information. All levels of government—federal, state, and local— keep pretty close tabs on how many people live in their areas. Plus, the federal census collects lots of demographic information on residents' ages, incomes, races, household sizes, and so on. The great thing about using demographic information is that there is lots of it; so much that it can be confusing. If you want to access this information, you can visit- the U.S. Census website http://factfinder.census.gov.

Many local governments will also make this information available for their communities, and many local chambers of commerce and newspapers will collect it as well.

Nail It Down!

Here are some steps to take to help you identify your industry and discover your target market.

Industry

You should have a solid idea of what industry you are in and the trends in the industry.

❑ Identify what needs, wants, desires, and problems your potential customers want to fulfill and solve.

❑ Identify what industry or industries you are in.

❑ Identify trends in the industry, such as changes in the market, technology, or government regulation.

❑ Identify the major players in the industry, both on a national and local level.

❑ Contact your industry associations to discover what benefits they offer; consider joining.

❑ Use some of these resources:

❑ For help in identifying your industry, check out:

http://www.naics.com

http://www.census.gov/eos/www/naics/

❑ For help in locating trade associations, visit these sites:

http://www.asaecenter.org

http://www.ipl.org/

Customers

There is an abundance of demographic information available for free.

❑ The U.S. Census Bureau maintains all the demographic records you are likely to need, although finding what you want can be confusing:
http://factfinder.census.gov

❑ Psychographic information is available for a fee. To get a taste of what is available, check out these sites:
http://www.esri.com/data/ersi_data/tapestry.html
http://www.claritas.com/MyBestSegments/Default.jsp
(look for the zip-code look-up button)

❑ Contact your city and state governments for local demographics, and check with local chambers of commerce.

❑ Talk to people who you think would be potential customers to discover what they think about your product, how much they would pay for it, how often they would buy it, and so on.

❑ Identify what needs, wants, desires, and problems your potential customers want to fulfill and solve.

❑ Create a list of potential features and benefits your product has and how these help the customer.

Chapter Seven

KNOW YOUR COMPETITION

W hat do you think it would mean if you wanted to start a business and, upon doing a little market research, you discovered that there was no competition? I mean, there was no direct competition, no one in your area offering your product or service? Would that be good or bad for you?

You might think that it would be good, because you would have the market all to yourself. But more likely it would be bad, because if you have no competition it means one of two things. First, that you have come up with a brand-new product or service that no one has ever thought of before. This is possible, but not likely.

The second, and more likely, explanation is that there has been a similar business to yours, but the owners discovered that there was not enough of a market to keep them in business. So sure, you'll have the market all to yourself, but it won't be enough, because it is too small.

It is very rare that a new business doesn't have competition. What is likely to happen is that your business will compete against already existing businesses, so there is no doubt that the field will be crowded. That's OK! Having competition will actually make your success more likely, not less.

In this chapter we'll look at why it is a good idea to get to know your competition, some ways you can learn from your competition, and how you can benefit from your competition.

LEARNING FROM YOUR COMPETITION

When it comes to learning about business, by far the best way to do it is by working in the industry you are entering, having someone else pay for your learning-by-doing. This is by far the lowest-risk way of learning about running a business. You don't risk your money because someone else's money is at stake. You don't risk your income because you have a steady job. And you get to see from the inside what kinds of mistakes a business can make. If you have the opportunity, I would strongly encourage you to try and get a job working for your future competition.

If you don't have that luxury, there are several ways you can learn from the competition.

Learn by Watching

First, you might do some competition shopping. That is, you would pretend to be a customer and then either call or visit the competitor to discover what its prices were, its customer service policies, hours of operation, and so on. You might actually purchase something, as well.

Second, you might do some behind-the-scenes investigating. For example, if your competitor has a retail location, you could sit in your car and watch how many people go in the store in an hour. Try to note their demographic and psychographic characteristics. See if they actually purchase anything. You can also talk to your competitor's customers to discover how happy they are with the products, prices, and service.

Learn by Asking

Finally, why not talk to the business owners themselves?

For example, you might try talking to competitors, asking them if their business keeps them busy, who their customers, are, and what sort of research they did before starting. You might find that even though there is a large market for your business, there is so much competition that it would be difficult for you to make money. But you are just as likely to find that there are areas of the market that the competition doesn't reach, niches that are open and that you can take advantage of.

Will your competitors talk to you? Chances are they will; it is largely a matter of how much they see your business as a threat. Now, if you are going to open a store right across the street from a competitor, they may not want you snooping around. But if this is the case, surely there are similar businesses that will not view you as a threat. Perhaps these businesses are across town, or even in another city. In fact, you are likely to find that most business owners would love to talk to you about their business, and indeed would welcome the opportunity to see you avoid the mistakes they made.

Types of Competition (Again)

Competition comes in two types: direct and indirect. Direct competitors are the ones that sell about the same thing as you, to about the same market as you. For example, for a bagel shop, other bagel shops are direct competitors if they are in the same area.

Indirect competitors are those businesses who solve the same customer problems that you do, but do it in another way. For example, an indirect competitor to a bagel shop would be the pastry shop down the road or the sandwich shop across the street.

Generally you should be most concerned about your direct competition, since it is usually these businesses that you can lose customers to. But you also have to be aware of your indirect competition because these businesses also form the industry that you are a part of. And as you saw earlier, knowing what is happening in the industry is essential to ensuring that you are not caught off guard.

Ultimately, you should identify and know your three main competitors inside and out. You should know their strengths and weaknesses, their customers, and how profitable they are. In addition, you should be familiar with your indirect competitors. Following them over time will give you insights into industry trends and allow you to spot who's getting ahead and who is falling behind.

COMPETITORS VS. COOPERATORS

Do you view your competition as an enemy to be crushed or as an ally who can help you in your business? Most small business owners will benefit from viewing their competition not only as competitors, but also as cooperators. Look at it this way: Let's say that you are pretty busy, so busy that you have to turn away business (may you have such trouble!). A new customer calls asking for help. What should you do? Tell them you're sorry, that you are too busy, and hang up? Wouldn't it be better if you could refer them to someone else in your business who you knew well enough to recommend?

If you turn the customer down, you lose, because you get no business, and the customer loses, too. But if you refer the customer to a competitor who does good work, everyone wins. The customer wins because they get their work completed. The other business person wins because they get to earn some money. And you win twice, once when the customer, impressed with your honesty and integrity, calls you in the future, and once when your competitor gets too busy and refers new customers to you.

Others do not have to lose for you to win. Often in small business everyone can win.

NAIL IT DOWN!

Here are some tips to get to know your competition better:

- ❑ Do as much competition research as possible before starting your business; you can learn from your mistakes or from theirs.

- ❑ If you have the chance, work for your competition before starting on your own.

- ❑ Being a customer of your competition is one way to learn from them; another is simply to do some research on them.

- ❑ Most business owners will be happy to talk to you if they don't perceive your business as a direct threat; they know that competition generally benefits all businesses.

- ❑ Try to get to know your competition so that you know who you can refer business to when you are too busy, and they to you.

Chapter Eight

KNOW WHAT SETS YOUR BUSINESS APART

When you go shopping, why do you buy the products that you do? Clearly, the ones that you buy represent the best value for you. But don't most people value the same things you do? Clearly the answer is no. If everyone valued the exact same things in the products and services that they purchased, all products would be the same. But even for products that essentially are the same, like cola soft drinks, people buy different brands. Why?

Because the companies that make these products do their best to make them different from one another, to make them somehow unique, to make them stand out.

Having your product stand out is often called "branding." For example, what do you think of when you think of Coke, or Ford, or Target? Chances are you think of these brand names the way they want you to think of them. They each stand out in a certain way.

Your product must stand out. If you offer exactly the same service as someone else, providing the exact same quality at the identical price, why would anyone buy from you instead of your competition?

In this chapter we'll look at some of the ways you can get your product to stand out, to make your brand unique.

WHY WILL CUSTOMERS BUY FROM YOU?

You must be able to answer this important question if your business is to succeed. No matter what you sell, you will want to offer your customers something a little bit different than your competitors. By managing the elements that surround your product, you can both make it unique and provide your customers with a way to think about your business. Once you decide what elements can be your strengths and which things you are going to leave to others, you can differentiate, or separate, yourself from your competition.

There are at least nine ways you can separate yourself from the competition (there may be more, and it will help your business if you can identify more). These nine are:

Traditional Marketing Mix	Other Competitive Elements
Product	Service
Price	Quality
Place	Prestige
Packaging	Innovation
Promotion	

The five elements listed on the left are called the Traditional Marketing Mix, or the 5 Ps. The rest are elements that can also set your business apart. We'll take a brief look at how each of these can make your business unique.

Product

Product is the good or service that you actually sell. What is it? How similar, or different, is it to other products?

By deciding what to sell, you essentially determine how much competition you will have. For example, if you wanted to go into the soft drink business, you could choose to compete against Coke and Pepsi by selling a cola. Or you could come up with a new type of soft drink with less competition. Many new companies will find it easier to produce a product with a difference rather than just a knock-off of an existing product. Having the difference gives customers another reason to buy, and companies can use it to justify a higher price.

Related to the actual product is the selection or variety of products that you offer. Often those offering a greater selection of similar products are stronger in the market because they can meet a wider variety of consumer needs, but this variety comes at a cost. Businesses offering more variety face higher production, shipping, and inventory costs than businesses concentrating on fewer choices.

Price

Sometimes solo business owners think that the only way they can break into business is by charging less than their competition. This is usually because they aren't aware of how they can use all of the marketing elements to set themselves apart or how these elements interconnect. As we'll see in the next chapter, solo businesses that try to compete on price alone often fail. Start thinking now about how you can make all of these elements work for you, not just price.

Place

In the days when most businesses had to have a physical presence, place really meant location. But today what matters is not where you are, but how you get the product to your customer, and that really means distribution. For retail businesses, their means of distribution is their place of business. For mail-order companies, catalogs and the mail are their forms of distribution. For someone who grows produce, a farmer's market may be their place. For an Internet company, the World Wide Web may be their place.

It is easy to see the trade-offs a business has to make with this element of the marketing mix. Having a retail location obviously limits your customers to those who can come to you. The barriers facing those wanting to open a retail store are fairly high because of the costs involved, which also limits how many can get into the business in the first place.

You might think that using other distribution channels, like mail order or the Internet, would free you from the limits of retail, but this also comes at a cost. Because the barriers to establishing a Internet-based business are lower, you are almost guaranteed to have more competition. So you can take your pick: limit your distribution or limit your competition. You can't have it all.

Knowing what ways your competition distributes their products, and how you might be able to distribute yours differently, may give you an edge. And if you do sell retail, remember the three most important things to look for in a site: location, location, location.

Packaging

This refers not only to the actual packaging that your product may come in, but also to all of the elements that surround your goods or services. If your packaging is fancy, you are saying that your product offers high value. If you have cheap packaging, you are saying that low price is important. For example, some breakfast cereals come in very fancy boxes and are high priced. Because many customers are price conscious, some cereals come in plastic bags and cost less.

If you sell a service, you also have packaging, but in a different form. Here your packaging might include things like uniforms that your workers wear, the literature that you send to prospective customers, or the hours that you are open. For example, if you received some sales materials that were full color and printed on glossy paper, what would your impression of the company be? What if you received the same information printed just photocopied on plain paper?

A good example of the packaging of a service business is car repair shops. These tend to fall into two categories: the higher-end car dealerships and the small, independent shops. If you drive into a dealership to have your car worked on, chances are you won't see a mechanic, and you certainly won't see any grease. You'll talk to a service writer, who will take your information and put protective covers on your car seat and floor. You'll pay near the high end for car work here.

If you go to a small car repair shop, chances are you'll talk to the mechanic directly, who will have grease on his overalls and certainly under his nails. However, prices will be lower.

Note how the packaging of each of these shops sends a message about themselves. The dealership says, "We are professionals, we treat your car with respect, we earn our higher price." The small shop says, "We work on these things every day and can answer your questions directly, and our low overhead means we can charge less."

Which is better? That's up to the customer.

Promotion

Promotion is more than just advertising; it is one of the essential ways you can market your business. Promotion is everything that you do to get the word out about your business, from how you answer the phone to the feel of your business cards. Promotion is so important that we'll dedicate all of chapter 10, *Know How to Reach Your Market*, to it.

Service

Service is just what you would think. For solo businesses, service usually means the hands-on, one-on-one type of service that is becoming more rare in today's market. If you go into a large supermarket or department store these days, you will find a large selection and low prices, but its service is often lacking. Why? Because high service usually means high price, and these stores have decided that their customers would rather have low prices and low service.

Excellent service is essential for most solo businesses to survive, because this is what they are selling. As we'll see, many small businesses have to charge a premium for what they sell, and superior service is what justifies their prices.

Plus, remember how we said that 80 percent of your business would come from 20 percent of your customers? You should treat those customers like gold, because they keep you in business. The general rule in the marketing world is that every happy customer you serve will tell one other person about your business. But if that same customer is unhappy with your service, he or she will tell ten others about his or her bad experience. You can't afford to have unhappy customers.

The exact level of service expected in your industry will be defined by your customers. For example, in some industries, having someone available 24/7 is expected. In other industries, if someone gets back to you within a couple of days, that's OK. One of your goals is to discover how much service your customers expect.

Setting Customer Expectations

When initially communicating with prospective customers, you will be in a great position to set their expectations. Often when you meet a customer for the first time, they're not sure what to expect. Will I be treated kindly? Will I get service promptly? Will the price be about what I want to pay? If I'm buying a service, will the job be done on time?

Since the customer doesn't know the answer to these questions, you can, and should, let them know what to expect. Setting their expectations can help you look good in your customer's eyes by making sure you can meet or exceed those expectations.

For example, if someone approached me about writing an article and asked how long it would take, I would ask some questions to find out more about what exactly they had in mind. Then, because of my experience in the field, I would know that the job would take, say, seven business days. But I would tell the customer to expect completion in ten business days. Why? For two reasons. First, if something unexpected comes up, say my dog gets sick or my computer crashes, I have a couple of days cushion to complete the job on time. If something bad happens and I do take ten days, the customer is happy because I met their expectations.

On the other hand, if I take the expected seven days or even less, the customer thinks I must be a real whiz to have exceeded their expectations by so much.

Quality

Those businesses that fail to offer high quality in today's market will not long prosper. You should assume that all of your competitors will offer a reasonably high-quality product or service.

Does that mean you should offer the highest quality possible? Probably not. Ask yourself, who defines what high quality means for my product? Me or my customer? It is always the customer! This can be a difficult lesson for many new business owners to learn. Chances are you've worked in a business that cut corners or hid flaws in its products and you swore never to do that to a customer.

Good for you! But remember two things. First, quality is always related to price. High quality means high price, if only because you will spend more time doing a quality job. This means if you offer high quality, you have to charge a high price, and if you offer perfect quality, you have to charge a very high price indeed.

Second, your customer may not care about getting the highest quality available. I've worked with customers who asked for quality that was well below my ability. This is a tough pill to swallow, so you have to ask yourself if you want to accept such work or not. Since it is the customer that defines what quality means, find out what quality means to them, and then exceed that.

Prestige

Some consumers will pay very high prices for items that they believe will set them apart from others. Why else would people pay $10,000 or $20,000 for a Rolex watch, for example, when a watch that keeps time just as well can be had for $10 or $20?

Prestige is usually directly related to price, and sometimes customers will confer status upon a product just because it is expensive. Convincing your customers that your product or service is unusual, unique, or likely to bring them status is an excellent way of justifying a higher price.

Innovation

Many industries are constantly changing, continually offering new products and services, or finding ways to reduce costs and keep their prices competitive. Successful business owners know they must constantly innovate or risk being left behind. Even those businesses that don't have to innovate will want to because innovation means higher profits.

What kind of businesses would not have to worry too much about innovation? The best examples are those trades that intentionally stick to the old ways, such as quilt making or handmade furniture. But even these businesses should still seek to constantly improve their back end, that is, the other tasks that they have to perform, such as record keeping, bookkeeping, and taxes.

NAIL IT DOWN!

Here are some questions to ask about how you can distinguish your business from your competition:

- ❑ Product: Is what you are selling unique, unusual, or special, or is it something that many others sell?

- ❑ Price: Competing on price is dangerous. What does your price say about your product?

- ❑ Place: How do you get your product to your customer? Can you think of an innovative way do this?

- ❑ Packaging: Everything that surrounds your product is packaging. What does your packaging say about your product?

- ❑ Service: For many small businesses, service is the most important key to success. How do you ensure that you are giving your customers everything you can?

- ❑ Quality: Your customers will demand high quality. How can you give them this quality and still make a profit?

- ❑ Prestige: If your product is uncommon or in high demand, what can you do to make it a prestige item?

- ❑ Innovation: All businesses will benefit from finding ways of doing business more efficiently. What can you do to reduce costs or increase income while maintaining or increasing customer service?

Chapter Nine

KNOW HOW TO SET YOUR PRICES

Finding the right price for your product or service is as much an art as a science. It takes a certain amount of guesswork and experimentation to find the one price that will maximize your income. But that doesn't mean pricing is a shot in the dark. Not at all. You should have a very good idea of what your prices should be before you actually charge them.

FINDING THE RIGHT PRICE TO CHARGE

The prices that you set will be influenced by three main factors:

- What your customers will pay.

- Your costs and expenses.

- Your ability to produce your product.

What Will My Customers Pay?

Everything for sale has a price that the market will bear. If you are selling something that the market is already familiar with, you have the existing prices to guide you. If you are selling something new to the market, you will have to do more research. But in either case, you can discover what price is appropriate fairly easily, using two methods.

First, if you have competition, look at what they are charging. If your competition can make a profit selling an item for a certain price, and if their expenses are in line with yours, you should be able to make a profit at that price, too. Plus, chances are that some competitors charge a very low price and others very high prices (think about cars, for example). This range in prices gives you a ballpark figure of where your prices might be profitable.

The second way to find an appropriate price is to conduct market research sales. This means actually making some small sales before you jump into business with both feet. The idea would be to conduct some business without all of the expenses of conducting business in earnest. You could experiment with your prices, find what the market would pay, and lose little, if anything, if it turned out that you couldn't make a profit.

Large companies do this all of the time—I've seen, for example, two catalogs from the same company with the same item listed at two different prices. They are trying to discover just how much people are willing to pay to maximize their profit.

Always remember that it is the customer that ultimately determines how much your product or service is worth. If no one is willing to pay the price you require, then you are out of business. But if they are willing to pay the price you ask, you can charge that and maybe more. Never be afraid of asking for what your product is worth—to your customers.

What Are My Business Costs and Expenses?
Just as what customers are willing to pay sets the ceiling for your prices, your costs and expenses set the floor. If you don't know what your expenses are, then the price you set may be too low. And if the price you set can't cover your

expenses, then you won't make a profit and you'll be giving away your product.

We'll look more at expenses when we discuss calculating your breakeven later in this chapter.

What Are My Reasonable Sales Goals?

In addition to finding a reasonable price, each business has reasonable sales goals that it can meet. In other words, each business can only be expected to produce so much or to have so much time for its service. It might be that you simply don't have the capacity to make or sell enough to make a profit.

Let's return to Betsy's Bagels as an example. Let's say that Betsy decides that she can only charge $.75 a bagel and keep her customers. Then the question becomes, how many bagels does Betsy have to sell to make a profit? It might turn out that she has to sell a thousand a day—is that reasonable for a one-person operation? Probably not. On the other hand, a large wholesale bagel business may produce and sell thousands of bagels per day with no problem. It all depends on the capacity of your business.

What happens if you can't produce enough to make a profit? You have a couple of choices. First, you could invest in the equipment or labor to increase your capacity, if you can afford it. Or you could find some way to reduce your costs and lower your breakeven (more on that shortly). Or you could find another, more profitable, business.

WHY YOU PROBABLY CAN'T COMPETE ON PRICE

Many solo business owners believe that they can break into the market by undercutting their competition on price. However, if there is one sure way to put yourself out of business, it is by not charging enough. There are three reasons that you have to charge the going rate, or more, to prosper.

Who Your Customers Will Be

Think about your own shopping habits. You would never buy everything solely on price, because you know that often a low price indicates lower quality, poorer service, limited selection, and so on.

So what kind of customer would you attract by offering low, low prices? Primarily those interested solely in price, the bargain hunters, those who care only about getting a deal. Well, that's fine, but after six months or a year you are going to discover that you are not going to be able to stay in business charging these really low prices. You can't because, as we'll see later when we do a breakeven analysis, you'll be losing money with every sale. So your prices are going to go up. Then what happens to your customers?

They have no loyalty to you; they only care about the deal. They'll be gone, and you will now have no customers at all. (On the other hand, if you start out charging a fairly high price and find you have to lower it a bit, do you think you'll lose many customers?)

You Want the Market to Want Your Product

Second, charging a low price makes it harder to get customers in the first place. What's the first thing you think when you see something advertised for an amazingly low price? Assuming that the item isn't stolen, you probably think that the quality must be terrible. And chances are you are right. As we discussed earlier, quality and price are usually related so that when one is high the other is as well and vice versa.

If you charge a low price, chances are you don't think your quality and service are bad, but how will you convince your customers otherwise? Charging a typical or even a high price sends a signal to your customers that your product is at least as good, if not better, than the competition.

Related to this is the issue of respect. I have seen situations where customers had very little respect for a business owner who charged very low prices. The customers would make unreasonable demands, abuse and insult the business owner, and treat the owner like she was lucky to have them as customers. Think about how you want your customers to treat you.

You Can't Compete with the Big Boys

Finally, you cannot charge really low prices because you will always have competitors who can and will charge less. There is a certain department store chain throughout North America that advertises that they always have the lowest price, and indeed they often do. But not everyone shops at this department store; in fact, there are about a dozen other department store chains across the country that compete very well by charging more. Why doesn't the cheapest always win? Because, as we mentioned earlier, not everyone always buys just on price. And what does that department store chain offer besides price? Sadly, very little. They can't afford to. Their service, selection, and quality are marginal.

In every industry there are businesses that do what this department store does: They sacrifice other things to price, and they do it successfully. Often these businesses are quite large, can take advantage of large economies of scale (meaning they can buy in huge quantities and therefore cheaply), and can promote themselves endlessly in the media.

But these businesses can't offer high quality and high service at the prices they charge. By being small, it is much easier for you to offer good quality and excellent service. But in return, you can, and should, charge a premium.

REVENUE, COSTS, AND EXPENSES

In order to know how to price your product profitably, you have to know what it costs you to produce your product and what your overhead expenses are. These factors will go into calculating your breakeven, which tells you what your floor price must be. In the next several sections we'll look step by step at how money flows through your business, and how this leads you to your breakeven, or floor, price.

Revenue

The money you receive in exchange for providing your good or service is called revenue. It is also often referred to as gross income, sales, or gross receipts. These all mean the same thing. Note that money coming into your business from sources other than sales, such as a loan or a tax refund, is not considered revenue and does not count as income.

Cost of Goods Sold

If you make or resell items, one of your expenses will be the Cost of Goods Sold (COGS). The COGS is simply the costs you pay directly related to producing and selling the item, including things such as raw materials, packaging, shipping, and labor.

Many small businesses fail to really calculate their cost of goods. Unless you take into account all of the items going into your product, including the cost of labor, you don't really know what it costs.

Your cost of goods calculation should include all of the relevant materials, ingredients, parts, and components of whatever it is you make. This includes things such as packaging, shipping costs, and the labor costs to manufacture the item. It does not include fixed monthly expenses.

If you run a service-based business, you may be wondering if you have a cost of goods. If you don't sell merchandise, then your only cost of goods is your time.

Expenses

Expenses are monies that you have to pay out to support or maintain your business. Some of these expenses will have to be paid every month or so, such as your telephone bill, your rent, and your insurance. Other expenses may be paid irregularly or as needed, such as what you pay for office supplies, advertising, or bank charges.

Not all money that goes out of the business checking account is considered an expense. Two good examples are the repayment of loan principal and owner's draws. The loan repayment is not an expense because it doesn't do anything to support your business. You are actually just returning the lender's money back to them. However, the interest you pay on the loan, which can also be viewed as the price you pay for the loan, is considered an expense. We'll discuss owner's draws in chapter 13, *Know How to Keep Your Books*.

Although cost of goods sold is a type of expense, it is calculated separately because it deals only with the cost of providing your product. Here's a way to keep this distinction in mind: If you went on vacation, closed your business doors, and made no sales for a month, would you still incur expenses? Yes! Those bills for the phone, rent, and insurance would still come due. However, without sales you would have no cost of goods sold, because you wouldn't have sold anything.

In addition to the ongoing expenses of running a business, you should have a pretty good idea of what your startup expenses will be if you haven't already begun making sales. For example, if you are planning on starting a business in the future, it would be great if you had estimates for your insurance costs, an advertising budget, the cost for permits and licenses, and an estimate of phone and utility costs.

Depending on the goals of your business, you should also try and estimate your quarterly expenses for years two and three.

CALCULATING PROFIT

Of course, when you generate revenue, you still don't know if you have profit, because profit means the money left over after you subtract your costs and expenses from your sales. And there are two different kinds of profit. Understanding the difference, and how you ultimately end up with net profit, is essential to having a successful business. No business owner can succeed without understanding the formulas described below.

When you do business, you take in money. The money you collect in exchange for your goods or services, before considering any expenses, we'll call your Gross Income (GI). This is the same as revenue or gross receipts.

To find our actual profit, we need to subtract our expenses from our GI, but we do this in two steps. The first step is to calculate the Gross Profit (GP). Gross profit equals gross income minus the cost of goods sold. Put into a formula, this would look like:

Gross Income – Cost of Goods Sold = Gross Profit, or

GI – COGS = GP

As an example, let's say that a company produces an imaginary item called a widget. The total cost of goods (materials and labor*) to produce a month's worth of widgets is $400. Our monthly income from selling widgets is $900, so the gross profit is $500. Put into the formula above we have:

GI	–	COGS	=	GP
$900	–	$400	=	$500

(*Note that a sole proprietor and single-member-LLC owners are generally not employees and do not pay themselves wages, so technically you do not have to calculate the cost of your labor in the COGS. However, if you want to take some money home at the end of the month, you had better calculate the cost of your time.)

Recall that the COGS is not the only type of expense we have. To calculate our final, or net, profit, we also have to consider our other expenses. To calculate net profit, subtract expenses from gross profit. Put into a formula, this reads:

Gross Profit – Expenses = Net Profit, or

GP – Ex = NP

Knowing what net profit is and how you calculate it is very important. Net profit is what makes the difference between a successful and unsuccessful business, and it is what you pay taxes on. You should know instantly what the term means.

Let's go back to the widget example. We've already calculated that the gross profit on widget sales is $500, but that isn't enough information to know if the company is making a net profit. The only way to calculate that is to also include its expenses. Let's say that its expenses are $100 a month. We now have enough information to make the net-profit calculation. Substituting the numbers into the formula for net profit:

GP	—	Ex	=	NP
$500	—	$100	=	$400

So our widget company is making a net profit of $400 per month. Converting our equations into a flowchart, the flow from income to net profit looks like this:

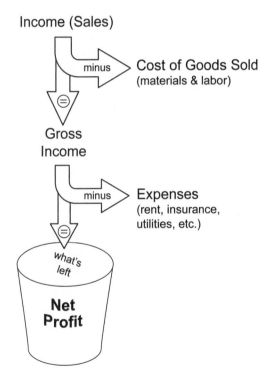

What you have left after cost of goods sold and expenses have been subtracted from sales is net profit

These formulas should suggest to you right away two ways to make more profit:

- Increasing your income (by raising your prices or selling more items)
- Decreasing your expenses (make your business more efficient)

For the rest of this chapter we'll look at two of the more basic breakeven formulas. First, we'll look at how you can calculate how much you have to charge to break even on your product. Then, for those who sell services rather than products, we'll look at calculating a service breakeven.

FINDING YOUR PRODUCT BREAKEVEN

When deciding how much to charge for your product, it is essential that you know the breakeven point. The breakeven is the price at which you do just that: You break even on the sale of the item. There is no loss and no profit. Your costs and expenses exactly balance your revenue. Therefore, to calculate your breakeven you will need to know both the cost of goods going into the item and your expenses.

Product Breakeven Formula

Here's an example of what this might look like with our widget example. Let's say the widget company had $900 in gross income, $400 in cost of goods sold, and $500 in expenses. What would its net profit be?

GI	—	COGS	=	GP
$900	—	$400	=	$500

As you can see, its net profit is exactly zero. If its income had been greater it would have had a profit; if its expenses had been greater it would have had a loss. The company now knows that its will either have to increase its income (by selling more or raising its price) or decrease its expenses if it is to make a profit.

Example Breakeven for Products

We'll discuss the two-step formula for calculating breakeven now. This can be a little confusing at first, so here's a tip. The answer we get for both cost of goods sold and gross income calculations will be in dollars per *each item* sold. We'll calculate our expenses on a *per month* basis. The breakeven result will be in the *number of items sold per month*. All of this will become more clear as we work through the example.

Step 1: Calculate Your Gross Profit

This is exactly the same formula we used when calculating profit earlier:

Gross Income – Cost of Goods Sold = Gross Profit, or

GI – COGS = GP

Recall that the gross income is simply the price that you are selling your item for, and when figuring COGS you should include the cost of labor as well as materials. However, unlike the example we used before, for breakeven we calculate the gross profit *per item* sold.

Step 2: Calculate Breakeven

This formula is new, and it calculates how many items you have to sell at the given price to break even, given your expenses. We'll divide our expenses by our gross profit to get the *number of items we need to sell per month* (assuming we're using our expenses on a monthly basis).

Expenses ÷ Gross Profit = Breakeven, or

Ex ÷ GP = BE

Example Breakeven

Let's look at a simple example. We'll use the company that sells widgets. Here's what we'll assume about the widgets:

Gross Income = $9 (each)

COGS = $4 (each)

Expenses = $1,000 (per month)

Step 1:

This is the same formula we used when discussing calculating gross profit.

GI	−	COGS	=	GP
$9	−	$4	=	$5

Step 2:

This formula calculates how many items you have to sell at the given price to break even, given your expenses.

Ex	÷	GP	=	BE
$1,000	÷	$5	=	200

In this example the company finds it has to produce 200 widgets per month to cover its monthly expenses. Once the owners know this, they can ask themselves, is this a realistic sales goal? If it is, and they know they can easily sell more than 200, then they can make a reasonable profit, because they only need to sell 201 to make a profit. If, however, producing or selling 200 widgets a month is unrealistic, they may have to reassess their business.

The breakeven formula is very powerful, because you can use it to play "what if." For example, what if your expenses were unexpectedly twice as high as you anticipated? What if your cost of goods were lower than anticipated?

Calculating Service Breakeven

Because service businesses don't create goods for sale but instead sell their time, calculating breakeven is a little different for them. The best way to calculate a service breakeven is to work backwards. First you decide how much money you want to make, then calculate how much you have to charge in the number of hours you can work during the year. As an example, we'll talk about Clyde, a computer consultant.

Step 1: Calculate Annual Income Required

Let's say that Clyde's goal is to earn a $40,000 profit his first year. This might be a challenging goal—we'll see. First we add Clyde's desired income to his calculated expenses for the year. We'll guess that his expenses will be $500 a month, or $6,000 per year (note that for this breakeven analysis we use annual figures). So the formula becomes:

Expenses + Desired Income = Income Required, or

$6,000 + $40,000 = $46,000

Step 2: Calculate Your Available Hours

Next, Clyde needs to figure out how many hours he would have available to achieve this goal. If we assume there are forty work hours per week, fifty-two weeks per year, there are 2,080 available hours (although many small business owners work much more than this). If Clyde takes two weeks vacation and ten holidays, he is looking at:

2,080 hours total – 80 hours vacation – 80 hours holiday = 1,920 available hours

Step 3: Calculate Your Billable Hours

For many service businesses, the number of billable hours, that is, the number of hours you can actually charge a client, isn't anywhere near the number of hours that you actually work. Clyde may find that he works eight hours a day, but he can only bill a part of that to a customer. He may need to go to the office-supply store, balance his books, prepare and send invoices, call on prospective customers, and prepare marketing materials, none of which is billable work.

As a rough estimate, let's say that in his first year of business Clyde can count on performing billable work about one-fourth of the day. Perhaps as he gains more experience this fraction will increase, but for the first year of many service businesses this is a realistic assumption (many people just getting into business are surprised at the low percentage of hours they can bill). So the formula becomes:

Total Hours Available x Percentage Billable = Billable Hours, or

1,920 x .25 = 480 billable hours per year

This may still be an optimistic estimate for his first year, simply because he hasn't established his business yet.

Now we have everything we need to know to calculate how much Clyde has to bill to make his income goal.

Step 4: Calculate Your Breakeven

Now we just take our income requirements and divide by the number of billable hours:

Income Required ÷ Billable Hours = Hourly Rate, or

$46,000 ÷ 480 = $95.83

Clyde would have to ask himself, is this a reasonable rate for someone in my business to charge? The answer is: It depends. If Clyde has special knowledge or a well-deserved reputation, this fee probably is reasonable. For less qualified computer consultants, it may be too much. On the other hand, if Clyde was an attorney, this fee would not be unreasonable at all.

Again, the breakeven formula suggests how Clyde can meet his goals. The first way is to simply reduce the amount of money he wants to make. Perhaps he can increase the number of billable hours he works. Or he might find reducing his desired income to $25,000 is more realistic. For example, if Clyde reduces his desired income to $25,000 but can work the same number of hours, the formulas become:

Expenses + Desired Income = Income Required, or
$6,000 + $25,000 = $31,000

Income Required ÷ Billable Hours = Hourly Rate, or
$31,000 ÷ 480 = $64.58

If Clyde is a run-of-the-mill consultant, this may be a more realistic hourly rate.

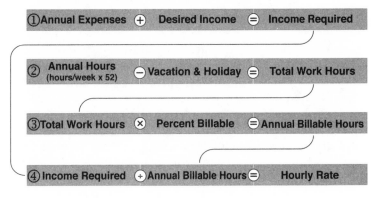

① Annual Expenses ⊕ Desired Income ⊜ Income Required

② Annual Hours (hours/week x 52) ⊖ Vacation & Holiday ⊜ Total Work Hours

③ Total Work Hours ⊗ Percent Billable ⊜ Annual Billable Hours

④ Income Required ⊕ Annual Billable Hours ⊜ Hourly Rate

Follow these steps to calculate a service breakeven

Other Breakeven Formulas

There are a variety of other breakeven formulas that might help you get a good idea of how much to charge. I won't go into them here because they only get more complicated. You can get these formulas from any business financing books, or your accountant can help you determine which would be the most appropriate for your situation (you do have an accountant, don't you?).

NAIL IT DOWN!

Here are tips to follow when establishing a price for your product or service:

❑ Remember that it is always the customer who determines what your product is worth, not you. Customers are suspicious of low prices as well as high ones.

❑ Finding the ideal price for your product is as much art as science; you may need to experiment.

❑ Unless you have a compelling reason to compete on price, you are probably safer charging a fairly high price; a small business is more likely to fail because they charge too little than because they charge too much.

❑ Know how to calculate your net profit; this formula is essential to business success.

❑ No matter what your product, you should know precisely what your breakeven amount is.

❑ If you have trouble calculating your breakeven, check with your accountant or a business advisor for help.

Chapter Ten

KNOW HOW TO REACH YOUR MARKET

arketing is one of the three essential legs that support your business. It has been said that if you build a better mousetrap the world will beat a path to your door, but if you don't tell the world about your mousetrap, how can they know to buy it from you?

For most solo businesses, marketing is nearly a job unto itself. Chances are you don't have a lot of money to spend on advertising, so you must decide carefully how to spend your funds. It's likely that you have more time than money, which means that you have to plan on hitting the pavement, going out and drumming up business on your own. Later we'll take a look at some opportunities for you to market yourself.

This might be a good place to let you know that solo business owners who can't or won't take the time and effort to market themselves have a very slim chance of success. If you are shy, reserved, or afraid to blow your own horn, you may be looking at a very long haul.

PROMOTION

Often when people think of promotion they think of advertising. This is normal because most of us are nearly swimming in advertising in one form or another: on radio, TV, the Internet, signs, in movies. So when it comes time to think about promoting your solo business, what's the first thing you think? Advertising!

For what it does, advertising is great, but advertising takes one thing you probably don't have a lot of—money, and lots of it. So in this chapter we are going to discuss the bigger picture, all of the various ways you might promote your product. Some are low cost, some are free (except for your time).

Everything you do related to your business is a form of promotion, from answering the phone to the feel of your business cards, from the way you dress to the name you choose for your business. Every exposure your business has with a potential customer affects your promotion.

Here's an example: A furniture-repair business is having trouble getting repeat business. So the owner decides that he should provide better service by placing more emphasis on communicating with his customers (we'll assume that he is already offering top-quality repair work). This service might come in the form of a quarterly newsletter, more frequent phone calls, or perhaps by cleaning up the shop so that it looks more professional (a form of packaging). As a result, there is more business, which then allows the owner to raise his prices and actually turn away some business. Turn away business? Isn't this foolish? Not in this case! Turning away business earns him the reputation of offering only the highest quality, which increases his prestige and also helps justify the higher prices.

In fact, in many situations, promotion is more important than any other single element in determining business success. Most of us know of situations where a business offered a mediocre product, had a high price without high quality, or offered a rip-off of another product and yet succeeded because it was able to promote it product more effectively.

As we said before, it doesn't matter how good your product (or quality or service or price, etc.) is; unless your market knows about it, they can't buy it from you.

Advertising

Promotion takes two general forms. The first is advertising. Advertising has several advantages and several very large disadvantages. Advertising is very good at reaching a large number of people quickly, especially to create awareness in the market. Think, for example, about how many people see television advertising, especially for nationally broadcast shows. Millions of people will see these ads, so they work very well at informing the market about new products and creating awareness that something new is available.

The Good, the Bad, the Expensive

There are several disadvantages to advertising, especially for a solo business. The first is cost. Generally, there is no such thing as cheap advertising. The cost of advertising is usually related to the number of people that it reaches. The larger the potential audience, the greater the cost. Those who sell advertising will try to impress upon you how many viewers or listeners or readers they have and why their form of advertising is such a good deal.

But consider another common problem with advertising: Many of the people who see or hear or read your ad have absolutely no interest in what you are selling. Recall the example of Betsy's Bagels. Although a lot of people may eat a bagel at some time, market research would show Betsy that the number who would actually be likely to eat her bagels was very small, perhaps only a few percent of those in the neighborhood. That means that if Betsy were to advertise to all of the surrounding community, perhaps 97 percent of her advertising dollar would be wasted.

The general rule of thumb in the marketing field is that half of your advertising dollars will be wasted; the key to advertising success is to identify which half.

Common Advertising Methods

There are lots of ways to spend money on advertising. Here are some examples:

- Broadcast media such as radio, TV, cable TV, Internet

- Print media such as magazines, newspapers, Yellow Pages, local "shoppers," phone directories, trade directories

- Other ideas such as billboards, direct mail, telemarketing, novelty items, signage

Advertising Tips

Here are three tips to keep in mind to help you decide whether or not to advertise.

First, as we saw in chapter 6, you must know who your target market is. If you choose to advertise with a medium that does not reach your target market, you are throwing your money away. Advertising salespeople will try and show you how your customer's demographics match their viewer/listener/reader's demographics. The problem is, if you don't know your customer's demographics first, you are likely to be persuaded that their customers are your customers.

Second, investigate where your competitors advertise. If you are selling a product or service to consumers, odds are pretty good that you may want to advertise in your community Yellow Pages if your competitors do. If your competitors don't, find out why not and find out how they promote instead. If you do not sell to consumers, but instead wholesale or sell to businesses, the regular Yellow Pages is a big waste.

Finally, you must track how new customers hear about you. If you don't ask your customers what brought them to you, you won't know what is working and what isn't.

Before conducting any advertising, call the media outlet and ask for a media kit. It will contain information on the cost of the advertising and demographics of their listeners/viewers/readers. Then, after you have established an advertising budget, you are in a position to plan your advertising. You should spread your dollars around to reach the most potential customers for the least cost.

Establish a Budget

It doesn't matter what kind of marketing you do, you should always establish a marketing budget before you begin spending money on marketing.

Many business owners find their marketing funds somehow disappearing quickly, and it's because they didn't plan their marketing campaign, they just started spending.

Get the prices for different marketing options, including business cards and brochures, and plan what you want to do.

PERSONAL SELLING

The other major type of promotion is personal selling. This is using yourself and others to market your business on a personal basis. Personal selling is in some ways the exact opposite of advertising because it is cheap, generally reaches only small numbers of people, and can be customized to the potential customer.

Also unlike advertising, which is often produced by someone else, you are the key to personal selling. Never forget that in addition to selling your product, with personal selling you are selling yourself. Many solo business owners have a hard time feeling confident enough to sell themselves in one-on-one situations, but those that do are among the most successful.

You might also hear this form of promotion called networking or word of mouth. Usually networking is when you, as the business owner, are out in public and tell anyone who will listen about how great your product is.

Here are some ways you can personally sell yourself and your product:

- Write press releases.
- Write articles in magazines or newsletters.
- Have an open house.
- Sponsor a seminar.
- Teach classes.
- Utilize social media.
- Give speeches.

GENERATING WORD OF MOUTH

When others talk about your business for you, you are using word of mouth marketing, and there is no doubt that it is the most effective form of promotion available. Companies spend millions trying to advertise things like movies, but if it doesn't get talked about favorably at work or among friends, no amount of advertising will help.

Word of Mouth Isn't a Strategy
Word of mouth is the most effective means of promotion you can get, but it is also one of the most difficult. You cannot simply say, "I'm going to promote my business using word of mouth," for the simple reason that you don't control it. Rather, good word of mouth is a by-product. It develops as a result of your running a great business that meets your customers' needs.

Fostering Word of Mouth
Here are some things you can do to help foster word of mouth. First, exceed your customer's expectations. How can you find out what your customers expect? Ask them! If you provide a service, ask them when they would like you to be

done. Often they will say something like "As soon as possible." This is an excellent opportunity for you to set your customers' expectations and then exceed them. If you tell them you can complete their job in a week, but then do it in four days, you have exceeded their expectations and made them happy. You have increased the chances that they will be return customers and tell others about you as well.

You should always try to create a good first impression with your customers and always avoid disappointing them. Sometimes disappointments are inevitable due to factors beyond your control, and if they occur, don't be afraid to tell your customer what happened. Don't make excuses, but instead tell them what you are going to do to fix the situation. No customer wants to hear an apology followed by, "But it wasn't my fault." Remember, customers want solutions to their problems, and they don't really care whose fault it is.

Another idea for word of mouth is to actively seek out criticisms and complaints. Have you ever seen those little feedback cards in a restaurant, where they ask you to rate them? They are looking for feedback so that they can find out what people don't like as well as what they do. Soliciting feedback can be effective for several reasons. First, if your customers feel there is a problem with your business, you want to know about it as soon as possible so you can fix it. Second, it is better to hear about a problem directly from a customer. You don't want a customer telling his or her friends about what a lousy business you run; it's better that he or she tells you directly.

OTHER WAYS TO PROMOTE

Promotion and marketing aren't limited to just advertising and word of mouth. Remember, everything you do is marketing. Solo business owners are their business. If you present yourself as friendly and helpful, people will perceive your business as friendly and helpful. Whenever you are in public you should be thinking about ways to market your business.

Find out if there are businesses or organizational meetings that you can attend, or find out if you could speak at one. Whenever you have happy customers, encourage them to tell their friends (remember, your customers' friends are probably also members of your target market). Perhaps you could offer some kind of incentive to customers to bring in new customers, such as discounts or coupons.

Ways to Promote Your Business

Here are some tried-and-true, along with some more novel, ways of promoting your business. Many of these are free or low cost. Whatever you do, you have to promote your business, and often the more original you can be the more effective your efforts. Be creative!

Coupons	Gift certificates
Stickers, labels, bumper stickers	Contests
Charity donations	Specialty items such as buttons or balloons
Community involvement	Fliers or brochures
Demonstrations or sampling events	Trade-publication articles
Yellow Pages ads	Window or sidewalk displays
Websites	Press releases
Grand opening/open house	Newspaper articles
Billboards	Videos
Business cards	Farmer's market/ flea market
Tradeshows/exhibits	Media advertising (TV, radio)
Sponsor a team	Adopt a Highway
Hats or clothing	Raffle
Sandwich boards	Vehicle signs
Church bulletin	Infomercial
Yearbooks	Social media
Home parties	Public speaking

Email	Race car sponsor
Join Chamber of Commerce or service organizations	Grocery bulletin boards

Marketing Materials Suggestions

Business Cards

Have you ever watched what happens when two people who are representing their businesses meet for the first time? After the handshake but before they depart, they will always exchange business cards. Business cards are your number one marketing tool. Once you have a business card, you should always, always have some available with you. You never know when you might run into someone who would be interested in your business, and it would be a shame if they couldn't contact you because you didn't leave a business card.

The first task of a business card is to tell the holder how to contact you. This means the business card should always include your name, address, and phone number. If you have an email address, that should be included as well, and a fax number if you use one.

You can influence the way your customers will view your business, so the other task for a business card is to reflect your business's identity. As such, it should be serious if your business is serious, like accounting, law, or security. It might be more lighthearted if your business is lighthearted, say for an entertainment business. If you have a logo on the business card, it should be easily remembered and related to the business.

Your business card must be easy to read. Most business cards have a light background with dark lettering. You'll find that the larger the business, the more conservative the business card. Why do you suppose this is? Large businesses have the resources to design the most distinctive cards, but they don't. Small businesses will sometimes design cards that are very distinctive, to the point of being obnoxious. Cards that are larger or smaller than normal, that are so colorful they hurt, or that have print that is difficult to read get attention only long enough to get discarded.

Online Promotion

Many solo business owners think that a site on the World Wide Web, along with social media, is their key to business success. They hear about other businesses exploiting online resources and figure they can do it too, especially since this can be quite inexpensive.

Don't count on it. While having a web presence can be inexpensive and add legitimacy to your business, taking advantage of the Internet is just like any other form of promotion—it has advantages and disadvantages and may not work as well as you hope.

Most businesses use Internet tools to reinforce or supplement their other marketing. They may use their websites to show detailed examples of their work, to have customer testimonials, or to provide more detailed features and benefits than a simple brochure would allow. They may use social media, such as Facebook and Twitter, to publicize new products or services.

Online tools can help you keep in touch with your customers in a way impossible just a few years ago. But while these tools can help your business communicate with your potential market, they can also absorb a great deal of your time. My suggestion would be, when creating a marketing plan, to explore the numerous options available to you online, then establish a goal for how much time you can spend, as well as money, on these tools.

Keep in mind that if it is easy for you to set up an Internet presence, it is just as easy for the thousands (or millions!) of others starting similar businesses. So while you might be expanding your potential number of customers by using the Internet, you are also dramatically increasing your number of competitors. And we come back to the basic question, why will your potential customers buy from you rather than your competitor?

Yellow Pages

For some types of consumer businesses, the Yellow Pages is still the first place to spend those limited advertising dollars. Think about yourself, for example. If you needed to find a plumber, a hair salon, or a furniture-repair business and you didn't have time to ask around, where would you look? For most of us the Yellow Pages, either the old paper version or the online version, is the place we go.

The question to ask to see if you need to be in the Yellow Pages is, do your competitors advertise there? If so, you should probably be there as well. If your competitors are there and you aren't, you won't have a prayer at getting a slice of the pie.

Make no mistake, the Yellow Pages are not cheap. Depending on factors such as the size of the ad, the market you are in, and the time of the year when you buy your ad (spring and summer are cheapest because the phone books usually are printed in the winter), you can be looking at $100 to $1,000 a month! Then ask yourself how many new customers you will have to get to cover that cost.

NAIL IT DOWN!

Here are some marketing rules of thumb and ideas for promoting your business.

Advertising

❑ There is no such thing as cheap and effective advertising.

❑ You should try to discover what your customers read, watch, or listen to before purchasing advertising.

❑ Advertising in the media, such as radio, TV or newspapers is very expensive; always ask for a media kit and compare how their customers' demographics match with your customers.

Personal Selling

❑ Personal selling can be very cheap and very effective, especially in small markets.

❑ Personal selling relies on your initiative and ability to get the word out more than money.

❑ You will generate word of mouth by providing an excellent value and superb customer service.

More Marketing Suggestions

❑ Try to be creative in promoting your business.

❑ Often the most creative ways of marketing your business are the most effective.

❑ If your competitors are in the Yellow Pages, you probably should be, too.

❑ Business cards are your number one promotional tool.

❑ Websites, social media, and other online tools are becoming an excellent way of showcasing your business and staying in touch with your customers, but you shouldn't rely on them to do all of your marketing.

❑ Create a marketing budget and stick to it; not only will you save money, but your marketing will be more effective.

Chapter Eleven

KNOW WHERE THE MONEY WILL COME FROM

Most businesses will require some money to get off the ground. Some people who sell services may not need much since what they sell is their time and knowledge. But many will need money to buy equipment, purchase supplies, and maybe get an ad in the Yellow Pages. Some will have this money available, some will not. Chances are pretty good that you will need more money than you currently have to start your business.

Money is often the hardest thing about business. It is hard to get, hard to hold on to, and hard to keep track of. Yet, money is the lifeblood of your business; you can't live without it. How can you get enough to get started? In this chapter we'll look at three ways you can get the money to get your business started, one way you probably can't, and we'll discuss some ways to get a bank to back you.

LENDERS

The first place most people think of to get money for a business is from a lender, such as a bank.

Lenders that make business loans earn their money by lending money to businesses that they believe will succeed. No success means no profit. They want your business to thrive. But at the same time, they need to reduce their risks; that's why they are so picky about who they lend money to.

If you do decide to approach a lender for a loan, keep in mind that not all lenders look for the same types of clients. If you get turned down for a loan, always ask why. It could be something as simple as the bank that turned you down doesn't make small business loans. It could also be that your business plan was missing an essential ingredient. If this is true, you'll appreciate knowing it so that you can fix the oversight.

We'll come back and look at how you can improve your chances with a bank later in this chapter.

FAMILY AND FRIENDS

Another source of money for many businesses is to borrow it from family or friends. I always tell people, if you want to lose a friend, go into business with them. Borrowing from people you know may be a good way to raise money; if you fail to pay it back, it may also be a good way to never see them again.

Another drawback to borrowing from family or friends is that sometimes they will lend you money and ask to be a "silent partner." This means that they want no involvement in the business—no work, no responsibility, no liability. But there are two problems. First, even if they have nothing to do with running the business, you should realize that legally they might have some responsibility if the business fails. If you have debts, your creditors will seek out any source of money for repayment, and whether or not the money was "silent" is irrelevant to them.

The second problem is that money brings power, despite what claims the investor makes. If your family or friends give you money and then begin to see it disappear, they may demand a role in your business. And this would go against one of your goals in running a business, that of being your own boss.

If you do decide to take money from family or friends as a loan, treat it as a business exchange because that is what it is. Draw up a contract, have an attorney look it over, and sign it. As we saw earlier, the main purpose of a contract is not to have something to prove the other party wrong in court, it is to avoid going to court in the first place.

Note that if you receive money from any source—family, friend, or relative—as a gift or inheritance, then you are free to do what you wish. The other party has no claim on this money.

YOUR SAVINGS

Finally, the first and best source for money for your business is to earn it yourself. Raising your own capital (the money you use to start a business) has three undeniable advantages.

- It is your money, you can do with it what you wish.

- If your business idea doesn't work out, you should be able to go back and earn that money again.

- Lenders are going to ask you to invest more than your time in the business; they also want to see your assets on the line.

If money is going to be a barrier to starting your business, begin thinking now about how much money you will need to start and how you will raise it. Many people get discouraged when they discover that they need money of their own to start their business. I've heard people say, "But if I just had $50,000, I know I could make this business work!" When I ask them how much money they have saved they say, "None."

When I ask what their credit is like they say, "Bad." It's like a carpenter who has never made a simple box asking for the resources to build the Taj Mahal.

No one is going to risk his or her money on a business owner who has a bad track record of managing his or her own funds. So if you need to, start saving and managing your own money wisely beginning today. It may take you longer to get your business off the ground than you initially hoped, but when you do it will be stronger and more likely to succeed.

OTHER SOURCES

Angel Investors and Venture Capitalists

You might have heard of these sources of financing for businesses, and they're out there. If your goal is to start a large software company selling cutting-edge computer services or a biotechnology company performing the latest in DNA research, these types of funders may be an excellent source of capital (and, by the way, you are probably reading the wrong book).

If you are looking to fund a small business such as computer-repair shop, a catering service, or an animal-grooming service, these types of investors probably aren't interested in you (and you are reading the right book!).

What about the SBA?

The Small Business Administration (SBA, http://www.sba.gov) is a government organization that helps create and foster small business through education and the facilitation of business loans. The SBA does not make loans directly; they simply assume some of the risk of a loan made by other lenders. In this sense they act very much like an insurance company.

When you go to a bank for a business loan, you will get the best terms if you can back the entire loan with your own capacity and collateral. But if the lender isn't convinced that your loan is a very low risk, it might turn to an SBA loan. By helping to guarantee the loan, the SBA frees the lender from some of the risk of taking on the loan and allows the bank to loan money to people who otherwise may not qualify.

Don't imagine that everyone qualifies for an SBA loan, though. You still have to meet their requirements, which in many cases requires more paperwork than traditional loans.

What about All Those Free Government Grants?

You might have heard that there are government grants available to people who want to start a business, money for the asking. Well, not really. The government never gives money directly to individuals. Instead, the government makes money available to agencies and institutions that then provide that money to their clients. For example, the SBA gives money every year to hundreds of Small Business Development Centers (SBDCs) around the country. These SBDCs then use this money, which it calls a grant, to serve their clients.

However, chances are this grant is going to be for education, not for starting your business.

Some government organizations and private entities do make grants available to some businesses in rather specific circumstances. For example, women and minority business owners can sometimes take advantage of grants, as can refugees from other countries. Note though that these grants are almost always to existing businesses, not to start-ups, so if you want a grant, you still have to get your business started the old-fashioned way, through hard work.

WHAT LENDERS LIKE

Remember, lenders such as banks are in business to make money, and they don't want to risk their money on a business they don't believe has a solid chance of success. To help evaluate the risk of lending you money, all legitimate lenders will look at several factors that help them judge if the business is a good risk.

Experience

Nothing can take the place of experience when it comes to judging how likely you are to succeed in business. Obviously a person with business experience, not just performing the work but also in managing the other aspects of the business, is a better risk than a person without this experience.

This doesn't mean that you have to have had a business to get this type of experience. Perhaps you had management experience in a job, managed a project to completion, or even managed your children and home finances. If you only have work experience in the industry, be prepared to explain how you will also manage your business successfully.

Collateral and Personal Investment

Generally lenders want to see that you are serious about your business and so will ask that you be willing to risk your own personal assets as a guarantee to the loan. Why should they risk their money on your business if you are not willing to risk yours? The amount that lenders like to see as an owner's investment will vary, but 20 percent is typical.

Collateral is another way you can help guarantee the loan, although some forms of collateral are better than others. Lenders love it when you own your own home and are willing to risk that; not only does it guarantee the loan but it shows you have a great deal of faith in your business idea.

A Business Plan

Lenders always ask for a business plan. They believe that if the business owner (that's you) doesn't have the patience and dedication to complete a business plan, he or she probably doesn't have the patience and dedication to run a successful business.

Many people shy away from attempting to write a business plan. They think it isn't necessary or that it simply takes time away from starting the business. And they are afraid of the hard work. Writing a business plan is time consuming and a heck of a lot of work. But I've helped people write business plans, seen them put in the hours of research and writing, and then seen their businesses get off the ground. Believe me, writing a business plan is a piece of cake compared to actually running the business.

Another reason a business plan is so important is that it forces you to plan and answer questions that every business will have to answer anyway. It is like designing a house. No one could take on the task of building a house without first creating a blueprint. If you wouldn't build a house without a blueprint, why would you try to build a business without a business plan?

Ability to Generate Cash Flow

Of all of the projections you make in your business plan, the one the lender will turn to first is the cash flow. The reason is simple. How will you pay back the loan if your business doesn't generate enough cash?

If you have been in business, be prepared to show a cash flow statement (as well as a profit and loss and balance sheet) for the past year or two of business. This will demonstrate that your business has done well in the past. And your cash flow projection should demonstrate that the business will continue to generate the funds required to pay expenses in a timely manner, including that loan repayment. We'll discuss these financial projections and more of what lenders look for in them in chapter 14, *Know Accounting Basics*.

Personal Credit History

Here's another example of how the lender will judge your business prospects by judging you. If you don't have a solid track record of managing your personal finances wisely, why should the lender think you will do any better with your business finances?

If your credit has been poor in the past but better recently, make sure that you let the lender knows this. Some lenders are willing to take a risk on business owners who have demonstrated that they have improved their financial management in the recent past.

Lenders will also ask for your personal financial records, such as tax returns, in addition to any financial statements you have from a business.

Business Demand and Competitive Advantage

As part of your business plan you'll be expected to explain why your business will succeed. You should be able to show that there is a demand for your product or service, perhaps by pointing out the success of the competition or by showing your own business success to date.

Also, you need to be able to show why your business is different than the competition. We already looked at this in chapter 8, *Know What Sets Your Business Apart*. Why will customers buy from you rather than from the competition? Are you open more hours? More conveniently located? Is your level of service higher? (I hope so.) Is your price lower? (I hope not.)

Character

In addition to your financial and business track record, lenders will also look at your personal track record. Do you have a positive history in the community? Have you worked with a lender or a bank before? Can you get good personal references from those in the community? Have you shown yourself to be a person who is involved, rather than just watching others?

Nail It Down!

Here are some factors to look at when evaluating where to get the money or capital to start your business.

Checklist: Lenders

❑ Evaluate your financial situation and create a budget outlining whether or not you will need a loan to start your business.

❑ Begin working on a business plan to demonstrate that you have what it takes to start and run a successful business.

❑ Develop financial projections showing how your business will do once it starts (more on this in chapter 14).

❑ Approach several lenders to evaluate how receptive they are to your business idea.

❑ Check with your state to see if any programs exist to help your type of business (Hint: most states have business-related websites where you can find this information).

Checklist: Family and Friends

❑ Check with the people you know to find if anyone has the money to loan you. Remember that a sure way to lose a friend or alienate a family member is to borrow money and not repay it.

❑ If you do decide to go into business with a friend or relative, treat it as a business deal, including creating a partnership agreement.

Checklist: Your Savings

❑ It's your money, you can do what you want with it!

Chapter Twelve

KNOW HOW TO MANAGE YOUR BUSINESS

Everything that gets done in the world happens because somebody does it. It may be carefully planned, it may be an accident, but nothing that humans do is done except by us. Granted, there are things that happen to us that we cannot control, such as the weather, but even during a hurricane, the way we respond is up to us. And I think you'll agree that the more we plan for the things we want to happen, the more likely they are to happen.

Planning and managing your business is what will allow you to achieve your goal. Without it, your chances of ending up where you want to be are unlikely. There are too many forces outside of your control that will take you along for a ride. But if you plan and actively try to achieve your goal, your chances for success improve dramatically.

WHAT MANAGEMENT MEANS

Management is a very broad term. It can mean many things, especially in business. But in general it means making the decisions for what you will do in your business.

For most businesses, "management" means you have to decide how to handle the issues that arise in three areas:

- Managing yourself and your time
- Deciding general business issues, including employee issues
- Money management

In this chapter we will spend most of our time talking about managing yourself and your time. We'll touch briefly on whether or not you are ready to hire employees. And of course, money management is so important that several of the following chapters are dedicated to that issue alone.

Managing Your Business

Small businesses are often started by people who love their work. A carpenter loves to build, a cook loves making food, a stylist loves cutting hair. Many of us are very good at what we do and seek a way to do it more productively when we own the business. But as we saw in chapter 1, running a business is much more than just doing the work. It also means finding customers, creating invoices, keeping track of the money, doing the taxes, managing your time and your employees, even taking out the trash. In other words, for most of us, running a business means wearing many hats, not just the one that we are particularly good at.

Think seriously about your skills in managing all of the aspects of the business. If you think you can handle them alone, great! If you can't, don't want to, or think it would be worth more to you to have someone else handle them, you should identify and plan for getting those tasks done now.

You should also think in some detail exactly how you will operate the business. For example, if you manufacture a product, you should be able to explain your supply chain, how much you will pay for parts or raw materials, the process you go through to create your finished product, and how your product is packaged and distributed. If you run a service business, you should be able to explain how customers will contact you, your hours of operation, and where and how you will see customers.

Listed below are some of the questions you should consider before starting your business. Don't be discouraged if you haven't already thought all of these things through. Take your time, set some goals and objectives, and find the answers to these important questions.

- Do you plan on working inside or outside of your home? If outside, what will the cost be?

- Do you have experience managing a business? Seeing projects through to completion? Working with others? Handling money?

- Do you have any significant barriers to success? If so, how will you get around them?

- Will you be the sole owner of the business? Will you have a partner? Employees?

- If you will have a partner, do you have a written partnership agreement?

- If you make a product, what is the process that you use to produce the product? Include descriptions of buying supplies, your production equipment, and manufacturing capacity.

- How do you distribute your product to your customers?

- If you provide a service, how does a customer contact you? How and where do you provide your service?

- What are your customer support policies? How do you solicit customer feedback?

- How much time do you plan on working? What are your hours of operation?

- How much money do you envision making?

- Do you have experts lined up to help you?

- Have you completed a business plan?

MANAGING YOURSELF AND YOUR TIME

Running a business of your own will almost always consume more of your time than working for someone else. If one of your goals in having a business is to have more free time, you should realize that this goal may take years to achieve. Someone said once that entrepreneurs (a fancy word for small business owners) are the only people who would prefer to work for themselves eighty hours a week rather than work forty hours a week for someone else.

This section presents a common planning system that can save you valuable time. It requires you to think about what goals you want to accomplish and then breaks down those goals into smaller pieces. Sometimes solo business owners are so overwhelmed at the amount of work facing them that they don't know where to start, and just freeze up as a result. The prospect of building an entire business from scratch is just too much to even consider.

But houses are constructed one piece of wood, one nail, one brush of paint at a time. There is nothing particularly magical about it, it is simply a matter of taking one step at a time, over and over. This is a process that will help break down many of the steps for you, using a method that first has you define your goals, objectives, and activities. Goals are the big picture, the destination. Such a goal could be "opening my business." The only way to make sure you are moving toward that goal is by setting shorter, intermediate objectives. To help meet your objectives, you can also define activities.

Here is an introduction to the steps you'll have to take to plan efficiently.

Set Goals

Every journey begins with a goal. If you don't have a pretty good idea of what kind of business you want to run, you should definitely define one before you start selling. You have to have a foundation before you can build a house.

Goals are the big picture, the large projects that you want to complete. Sometimes it isn't clear how to start achieving your goals. The best way is to break down a large goal into several smaller ones. Breaking a large goal down into smaller steps makes accomplishing your goal easier because it gives you a roadmap to follow, and you can feel good about completing each step along the way.

Goals are sometimes fuzzy. That is, it may not be clear to you exactly when you have achieved your goal. For example, if your goal is to start your business, have you achieved it when you earn your first dollar, when you make your first sales call, or when you get your permits? Having fuzzy goals is OK; we'll talk about how you can use these intermediate steps to help you chart your way toward your goal.

Goals can be short term or long term. You should put together some of both. You might have a couple of three-year goals for things that you would like to achieve, as well as some shorter-term goals, say six to twelve months. Completing these short-term goals should help you reach your long-term goals.

Establish Objectives

Objectives are the actual steps that you have to accomplish before you can meet your goal.

Unlike goals, which can be a bit fuzzy, objectives are always concrete, measurable, specific, and usually timedefined. You can always say with certainty if you have or have not completed an objective. Continuing our example above, if your goal was to start your own business, some of the objectives you would have to accomplish would include obtaining your permits, making sales calls, and earning your first dollar. Notice that you can say with absolute certainty whether or not you have done these things. You either have or have not done them.

You will want to break goals into several smaller objectives; establishing two to five objectives per goal is common.

Plan Activities

Planning activities means that you break each objective into the small, sometimes trivial, details that must be completed before the objective is accomplished, things like calling people or going to the store. Usually each objective will require from two to five or so activities.

It is an excellent idea to give yourself a written deadline for completing the activities. Once you have built up a set of activities along with completion dates, you can use the dates to create a to-do list to help you plan what to do on specific days.

Set Priorities

You must not only determine which activities you will need to accomplish before you can achieve your objectives and goals, you must set priorities on those activities. Some things you just have to do today. Others can be put off. When starting a business, there are some things that can't be avoided.

Registering your business entity or getting the state permit to sell goods is a task that must be completed before you start making sales. When you are running your business, you'll find that many things demand your attention at once, but you can only accomplish one task at a time.

You'll need to set priorities to determine which task is most important, and then set aside the time required to complete the task. Remember that tasks usually take longer to complete than you initially expect. Set aside more time than you think you'll need, unless it's a task that you've done many times before. Taking a few minutes each day to plan the tasks for the day or the week could save you hours of wasted time later on.

Time Management Tips

Plan
Unfortunately, many business owners feel rushed because they think they are too busy to plan. In fact, if they would take even five minutes a day to plan for what is ahead, chances are they could get more accomplished and actually have more free time. It isn't uncommon for you to get an hour or two in return for ten minutes of planning. Remember, a good plan is like a blueprint: It tells you what to do, when to do it, and allows you to make mistakes on paper, rather than for real.

Do Tough Stuff First
Most of us have an aversion to doing hard or unpleasant work. One strategy for getting the tough stuff out of the way is to do it first. Make a list of the things you need to do, and then do the thing you like the least first. Author Brian Tracy calls this "eating the frog," because after you eat the frog

everything left tastes great. In the same way, once you get the really unpleasant work out of the way, the rest of the day will seem like a joy.

Set Limits

A related strategy to doing the tough stuff first is to set a time limit for doing things that you don't like. For example, if you don't like keeping your books, you might make a point of planning to work on your books for thirty minutes, first thing every day. Setting that thirty-minute limit means that the pain won't be too overwhelming. You know you can handle it for that long, and if you discover that it isn't as bad as you had imagined, you might just go for another thirty.

Learn to Say No

One skill every successful business person has to acquire is the ability to say "no." People will ask you for favors, to do work at a reduced rate or for free, or to contribute your time for a worthy cause. Learn to set limits and say no.

Here is one suggestion for making this easier. Every year, establish a budget for how many charitable or community projects you can take on. This budget might be in terms of hours or dollars, it doesn't matter. The point is, having a budget lets you contribute your talents, but also gives you a way to say no when you have to. When others approach you for time or money, evaluate their request and see if it fits within your budget. If not, tell them so.

This same principle applies to business as well as charitable ventures. If you are too busy you should look at two things. First, evaluate raising your prices. Next, if you don't think you can take on more work, pass the referral on to someone you know who can do a good job. You don't do anyone any favors by stretching yourself too thin and doing a poor job for a customer.

Write Things Down

Not everyone benefits from having a fancy to-do system, an appointment book, or a personal digital assistant. But everyone, and I mean everyone, has to have a way of keeping track of notes, writing down appointments, and keeping things on paper. You will never succeed if you don't. Find a system that works for you and use it.

Establish Priorities

It always seems that there are more things to do than there is time in the day, and this is doubly true for business owners. You will never accomplish everything you could do, so you need a way of identifying the things that are most important. As part of your everyday planning, prioritize what must be done, what should be done, and what you would like to do, and write it down.

There is nothing wrong, by the way, with scheduling free time or vacation time along with work. Sometimes people get so caught up in their business that they forget that recreation is essential, too.

TAKING ON EMPLOYEES

I'm guessing that most of the people reading this book are interested in starting solo businesses, with one person. Some of them will grow larger in time and need to take on employees, but for this book we are going to concentrate on having you run your business solo.

Most small business owners who have employees agree that the single biggest problem running their business is their employees. So, how can a business owner know when he or she should take on additional help? Here are a few things to think about:

Do you know exactly what you want the employee to do? Can you develop a thorough, written job description? It isn't good enough to say that you are too busy to handle all of the business tasks yourself. You should have specific duties for the employee in mind before you hire.

Could you hire an independent contractor or temporary worker instead of an employee? An independent contractor runs his or her own business, so you don't have to be responsible for paying taxes or worrying about hiring and firing laws. ICs usually work for a specific amount of time and then are done. However, as we saw in chapter 5, *Know Your Rights and Obligations*, the tax laws concerning hiring ICs are strict because some employers try to claim employees as ICs and avoid paying taxes.

Temporary workers are actually recruited, interviewed, hired, and paid by a temporary-worker agency, and they work "on loan" to you. You pay more per hour for a temp worker than an employee, but if your needs are limited, this can be a cost-saving option.

Will hiring the employee allow the business to earn more money than he or she costs, and can you afford to pay him or her? These are actually two separate questions. If an employee can't generate additional revenue or free you to generate additional revenue, how will you pay him or her? Even if you can't get your current work done in the time you have, hiring an employee that doesn't generate revenue will put you out of business as surely as not having enough work. Even if your employee can generate enough revenue to justify bringing him or her on, will you have enough money to pay him or her until that revenue comes in? It might take several months to bring the employee up to speed, or between when the work gets done and when you get paid for it. Can you afford to carry the employee until that money comes in?

Do you want the hassles of recruiting, interviewing, hiring, training, paying, and possibly firing employees? There are many, many laws that you have to follow when taking on employees. We won't address them here because they are so complex. Most small business owners will engage their bookkeeper or accountant, or hire a payroll service, to help with the paperwork and legalities of hiring and paying an employee.

Nail It Down!

Here are the key elements to remember for managing your business:

❑ You should have a good idea of how your business will run day to day: Who will do what, where you will buy supplies and equipment, etc.

❑ Managing your time is essential for success. Follow these basic steps:

❑ Set general goals for yourself

❑ Establish objectives

❑ Plan activities

❑ Set priorities

❑ Planning is key to management. Write things down!

❑ Taking on employees may be one of the more complex things your business may do. Make sure you really need an employee and explore other options if you aren't sure. Plus, remember to get expert advice.

Chapter Thirteen

KNOW HOW TO KEEP YOUR BOOKS

One of the most common mistakes that small business owners make is not understanding or carefully tracking their finances. Too many businesses use only one tool to handle their money: their checkbook. And while your business checkbook should be the heart of your bookkeeping system, it is only the start.

This chapter isn't going to make you a bookkeeper. Instead, its goal is to make you familiar with a typical bookkeeping system so that you can either establish your own system or gain the knowledge to hire someone to help you.

BOOKKEEPING VS. ACCOUNTING

To get a complete picture of the financial health of your business, you'll need to look at it from several different viewpoints. Just as you can't know what the inside of your house will look like by looking at the outside, you'll need several different viewpoints to get a complete picture of your business finances.

Bookkeeping

Of course you have to keep track of all of the money that comes into and goes out of your business. Not only is that the only way you can know if you are profitable, it is also how you will determine how much you owe in taxes. Keeping track of your day-to-day finances is bookkeeping.

Bookkeeping concentrates on the individual transactions that your business does every day, including keeping track of the paperwork that goes along with those transactions.

Think of it this way. If you were lost in the forest, you could easily see how healthy the trees were, but you would have no idea where you were in relation to the entire forest. If you were in a helicopter flying above the forest you could see where you were but would have no idea of how healthy any individual tree was. Bookkeeping is like looking at each tree; you see the details at the expense of the big picture.

Accounting

Accounting is like being in that helicopter; you get the big picture at the expense of the details. The accounting process takes all of those daily records you generate (your bookkeeping) and distills them down into three formats that show you the financial health of your business. You need both thorough bookkeeping and accurate accounting to really know what is going on.

We'll take a look at accounting in more detail in the next chapter.

BOOKKEEPING OVERVIEW

Dangers of Not Keeping a Handle on Finances

Imagine that you suddenly got the chance to coach your favorite sports team. But you were given little time to prepare. There you were, on the sidelines, with no clue about how much time was left in the game, who the players were and their relative strengths and weaknesses, or even the score in the game. Plus, you didn't know anything about your opponents. It would be difficult, if not impossible, to win that game, much less plan for future games, without having the required knowledge.

As ridiculous as this scenario sounds, this is the situation that many business owners find themselves in. They have no idea whether or not they have cash on hand, don't know what kind of profit they are making (or even if they have any profit at all), and don't know what the business owns and owes. In other words, they have no idea if their business is succeeding or failing. Obviously, if you want your business to succeed, you have to have a handle on how well it is doing financially. Money may not be your only goal in running a business, but it is an essential element in any business's success. Money is the lifeblood of a business—lose too much and you're dead.

You don't have to get caught in this trap. By following some simple, time-tested guidelines, you can help ensure that your business works for you. There are four great reasons for you to stay on top of your finances.

Management

One of the elements in managing your business is managing your money. You couldn't very well manage any employees you had unless you knew where they were at all times and what they were doing, so how can you manage your money unless you know how much you have, where it is, and what it is doing? Actively managing your money will allow it to work for you and reduce the inevitable stress associated with not having enough on hand at all times.

Taxes

Here's a question for you. Who is responsible for calculating how much you owe in taxes? It isn't the government, it's you.

You keep track of your income and expenses, and then use the tax law to calculate how much tax you owe at the end of the year. Obviously, you don't want to pay too much; that would be foolish. On the other hand, you don't want to pay too little; that would not only be illegal, but you would also be cheating those of us who do pay our fair share. Oh, and if you get audited, you have to demonstrate to the IRS that your income and expenses are legitimate and the taxes you have paid are correct.

Financial Assistance

If you decide to seek financial assistance, such as a loan, chances are excellent that the financial institution will ask for a copy of your financial records. If you've been in business a while, they may ask for up to the last three year's records. They do this simply to see how well you have run your business and to get a good feel for how well you manage your money. It's just like if you bought a used car, you would want to see the previous owner's maintenance records to verify that the car was, as they claim, well cared for. The lender wants to make sure that your business is also well cared for before it puts its money at risk.

Theft

If you read the local newspaper at all, you've undoubtedly seen articles about embezzlement from small businesses. It happens with amazing regularity. Often, a person is hired at a small business to handle the books, sometimes on a part-time basis. He or she is given the ability to write checks and often to order supplies. Over the course of months, he or she ends up stealing business funds and siphoning off money into his or her own pocket.

A common method of embezzlement is for bookkeepers to set up shell companies, which means they open checking accounts for businesses that do not exist, and whose accounts they control. Next they create phony orders from these phony companies, supposedly placed by the company that they work for (that would be your business). Since they can write checks from the business account, they pay the phony company funds from your business for these imaginary orders. The money actually goes to them.

Without proper oversight, it is surprisingly easy for this type of theft to go unnoticed, and many embezzlers never get caught. Even when they are caught, they rationalize their acts, saying they meant to pay the money back. They never do.

There are plenty of other ways that unscrupulous employees can rob you blind. You should take some common sense steps to protect yourself. First, it is always a good idea to be familiar with accepted bookkeeping practices so you can see if someone is doing something out of the ordinary. Second, you could consider making your signature a requirement on all checks, or perhaps on all checks over a given amount, rather than give someone else this power. This would help ensure that you are aware of where checks are going. Third, if you do hire a bookkeeper, be sure to check his or her background and references. One phone call might save your business from ruin.

Three Rules for Brilliant Bookkeeping

For simple businesses, such as a single-owner business with no employees, keeping your books can be very simple. But as soon as the business becomes more complicated, the business's finances quickly become more complex. You will certainly want to discuss your business's bookkeeping and accounting needs with an expert before you begin. But regardless of how complex your business is, the basics still apply. You must follow these rules.

Keep All Business and Personal Finances Separate

Here's another experiment to think about. You open a new deck of cards. Which would be easier—to separate the cards by suit when they are already with one another or to shuffle the cards, throw them up in the air, and then separate the cards by suit? Clearly, separating the cards at the beginning, when they are already with one another, is easier than when they are all mixed up. And that is the reason you want separate business and personal checking accounts.

I don't care how small your business is, you want to keep your business money and your personal money in separate pots, and that means having separate checking accounts. The checking account is the heart of any business's money-management system, and it is unrealistic to think you could run a business without one. You can do it; there is no legal requirement that you have two accounts. But at the end of the year when you are searching for business-related tax deductions, you'll be going through your single checking account and trying to remember what your checks were written for. Was that check to the office supply store for business materials or construction paper for your kid's school project? Having separate accounts saves time and prevents you from making costly mistakes.

When you need to take money out of your business for personal use, you can write yourself a check from the business account to your personal account. This is the owner's draw that we'll discuss shortly. If you need to inject money into the business from your personal funds, write a personal check to the business (this is a perfectly legitimate thing to do). In each case you leave a paper trail of where the money comes from and where it goes. Without leaving such a trail, you can't be sure of where your money is going, and you can't be sure of just how much of that income and expense is taxrelated. If you are ever audited, the IRS will expect to see a separate listing of personal and business finances, and keeping your books this way from the beginning is much easier than trying to separate them in a hurry.

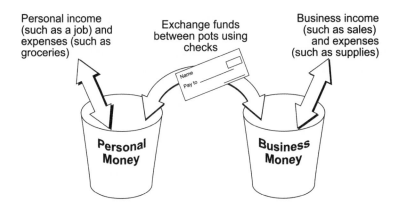

Personal income (such as a job) and expenses (such as groceries)

Exchange funds between pots using checks

Business income (such as sales) and expenses (such as supplies)

Personal Money

Business Money

Keeping your personal and business funds in separate accounts lets you track your finances more efficiently

Maintain Your Books Regularly

You'll need to update and maintain your books regularly. Depending on how frequently money goes into and out of your business, this may mean daily, weekly, or at the most, monthly. Few businesses, especially in the first years, can afford to ignore their books for more than a few days. For most businesses, keeping your books up to date means:

- Depositing checks as soon as possible and recording them in the register.

- Recording all transactions, including cash, on a regular basis (preferably daily).

- Billing customers promptly with the payment terms printed on the bill, and then tracking which customers are billed when so that you know which bills are overdue and which have been paid.

- Recording expenses when they occur and keeping receipts for tax purposes.

A good rule of thumb is that you should have a good idea of how much money you have in your business checking account, to within a few dollars, **at all times**. This tracking of funds into and out of your checking account is your cash flow, and it is so important we'll talk about it at length in chapter 14, *Know Accounting Basics*.

Keep Copies of All Records

The paperwork that you generate in your business from daily transactions are called the general records, or source documents, and it is important that you keep them for several reasons:

- To help manage your business. You can't tell where you are going if you don't know where you are.

- To help you prepare your financial statements, which tell you how well your business is doing throughout the year.

- To help in preparing your taxes at the end of the year. To calculate your taxes owed, you will need to know where your money came from. To justify your business deductions you'll need to know where it went.

- Finally, if you are ever audited, these records will be required to prove to the tax agency that your tax return was correct.

The requirements for retaining your records will vary state by state, but a good general rule is to keep as much paperwork as you can for as long as you can. Of course, this isn't always practical, so you should consult with the IRS and your state taxing agency to get the statute of limitations for your situation. Many experts recommend that you keep your original or source documents up to seven years. But you should keep copies of your filed tax returns forever. For more information, see IRS Tax Publication 583, Starting a Business and Keeping Records.

Elements of Bookkeeping Systems

The Heart: A Business Checkbook

The heart of any small business bookkeeping system is the business checkbook. It is unrealistic to think that you can run a business without a checkbook. You could do it, but you wouldn't want to. You would end up wasting time and money, and your chances of making a costly error would be very high.

If you already have a personal checking account, get another account for your business. If you use the business name for the account, your bank may want to charge you more than for a personal account. Shop around—try to find a free or low-cost business checking account. You will probably have to have an EIN before you get a business checking account—we'll cover those in chapter 15.

In addition to your checkbook, you'll have to keep all records and receipts that your business generates. Try to develop a system that will let you retrieve your records quickly. Depending on how much paperwork your business generates, you might be able to get by with an accordion folder with twelve divisions. Each month you would put all of your records into that month's section. More complex business will require more complex ways of keeping track.

More Sophistication

If your business is more complex, you'll need more complex accounting methods to track your progress. If you extend or receive credit, you will have to use accounts payable and accounts receivable so that you know who owes you money and who you owe money to. We'll talk more about these in chapter 14.

If you sell merchandise, your business must track the inventory you buy and sell. You'll have to do this for tax reasons, as well as to know what you have in stock. Tracking inventory can be complex if you have lots of items.

If your business has employees, you must keep track of your payroll and payroll taxes. This again can be quite complex, and many businesses get into tax trouble because they do not pay enough attention to this essential part of their business.

If your business has more than a few employees or is doing significant business, you should probably use a more complex accounting system, including ledgers and the double-entry bookkeeping system. We'll talk more about that in the next chapter.

Here is a chart showing what kinds of accounting tools you should use depending on the type of business you run.

If your business . . .	You should use . . .
Is in business	• Checkbook (a must for any business!) • Records and receipts • Income and expense journals
Extends or receives credit	Accounts payable and receivable
Sells merchandise	Inventory records
Has employees	payroll records
Needs more control	Ledgers (double-entry system)

PAPER VS. COMPUTER

As I mentioned in chapter 4, lots of aspiring business owners think that they won't have to worry about their bookkeeping and accounting chores because they'll have the computer do all of the work. And in one sense, they're right; computers can relieve you of a lot of the grunt work involved in maintaining your books and charting your finances.

But computers, like any tool, are only useful in the hands of a person who has the knowledge and skill to operate them. To see if you are ready to use a computer in your business, think about these two questions:

- Do you have a clear understanding of general computer usage now?

  For example, can you surf the web, send email, and copy and paste text? If so, you probably know enough about the computer to get by.

- Do you have a good handle on bookkeeping basics?

  For example, do you currently balance your checkbook regularly, tally your income and expenses monthly, and understand what a cash flow is? If so, you probably know enough about bookkeeping to go electronic.

If you couldn't answer yes to these questions, you should probably delay using the computer for your bookkeeping until down the road. You will probably have enough on your hands to keep yourself busy without having to worry about learning the computerized bookkeeping software, and until you do there are plenty of paper-based solutions available at your office-supply store.

Computer Options
Although keeping your books on paper is often a great option for small businesses, many solo business owners will want to start their books using a computerized solution right away, either because they already have the skills or because their business is sophisticated enough to make the software solution more efficient in the long run. Here are some of your options when it comes to computerizing your books.

Spreadsheets

If you are familiar with spreadsheet programs, like Microsoft Excel, you can easily create simple spreadsheets to keep track of your income, cost of goods, and expenses. The spreadsheet can then automatically do the math and calculate things like gross income and net profit. Lots of templates, with the math functions and charting macros abilities already in place, are yours for the finding on the Internet.

Bookkeeping Software

Software packages that allow you to enter and track not only financial information, but also things like inventory, billable hours, and employee payroll. These packages can save you plenty of time if you have the expertise to use them.

Simple checkbook programs, like Quicken or Mint (an online option), may be all you need if you run a service business. These programs not only do the math, they can also print checks and generate monthly reports.

Many business owners use QuickBooks, which is a powerful program that can handle the bookkeeping and accounting needs for just about any business. Many similar programs are also available, such as Peachtree and AccountEdge.

My suggestion would be to consult with your accountant before investing in such a program. Your accountant may be able to work with you, and even offer training, on a package that you can use in coordination with them to make your bookkeeping easier and more efficient.

THE THREE MOST IMPORTANT WORDS

Chances are you are already confused with a lot of this money talk. Most business owners are. Nearly every business, from a simple dog-sitting business to a complex car dealership, will be more successful if it follows these three words when it comes to managing its money and keeping a handle on its financial health:

Get Expert Advice

As we saw in chapter 4, *Know Who Will Help You*, hiring outside help often ends up being cheaper than trying to do the work yourself, and of course there is no question that a bookkeeper or accountant knows more about his or her field than you do. (If you knew more than the expert advising you, you either have a poor expert or are in the wrong line of work yourself.) You might want to review this section and start shopping for a pro to help you.

So, How Do I Pay Myself?

If you have worked for someone else, you have been paid a wage, which includes your hourly pay minus whatever taxes and other deductions you owe. By law, all employees are paid wages. But when you work for yourself, you usually are not an employee of your business. This means that you do not pay yourself a wage. Instead you will withdraw money from the business's net profit for your own personal use. This is called an owner's draw. (In this discussion we are assuming that your business is a sole proprietor or LLC—if you have a corporation, chances are you are an employee and do pay yourself a wage.)

If you have employees, you have to pay them; the government gets very upset when wages and taxes aren't paid (the employees won't be too happy either). But as a sole proprietor or LLC member, you not have to pay yourself. An owner's draw is completely optional. You can take out whatever is in the business account for personal use, or you can leave it in. As we'll see in a minute, it doesn't matter to anyone except you how much of an owner's draw you take. But of course, if there is no net profit from which to take a draw, then you don't get one.

An owner's draw is the money you take from the business to spend on your personal needs, such as groceries and recreation. Here's the tricky thing to understanding an owner's draw. The money you take out of the business as an owner's draw is already your money—you are simply moving it from one pot to another. Here is how the process works.

Remember when we discussed how you figured out your net profit? We used these formulas:

Gross Income (or Sales) – Cost of Goods Sold = Gross Profit

Gross Profit – Expenses = Net Profit

Looking at how your business money flows, you find your net profit like this:

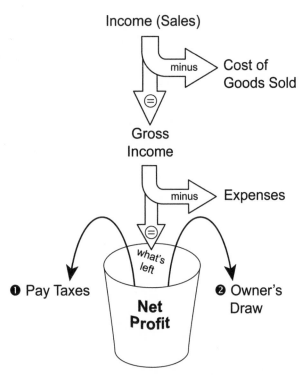

An owner's draw is money you take out of the business for personal use. Because it comes out of the net-profit bucket, the money is already yours and has no tax implications.

The net-profit bucket is the total sum of what your business makes, but that doesn't mean all of the money in this bucket is yours to spend as you please. Instead, several things have to be taken care of before you go out and buy that boat you've always wanted.

First, if the level of net profit in your bucket is high enough, you will have to pay taxes out of it, such as your self-employment and income taxes. Many novice business owners neglect their taxes and forget to set aside some of their net profits so that, come tax time, they don't have enough in reserve. Cheating the IRS is not a good way to build a successful business. (Taxes are complicated enough that you will want to get some expert advice on how to keep yours as low as possible.)

Second, you will want to keep a fair amount of money in your business's net-profit bucket to put back into expanding your business, act as a cushion against unforeseen incidents, or to take advantage of unusual opportunities.

Finally, if there is money still left in your bucket at the end of the month or the quarter, you can take an owner's draw. You do not have to take a draw, and many business owners don't take a draw for several months, or even years, while they establish their business.

Taxes on Business Income

As we'll see when we get to chapter 15, *Know How to Minimize Your Taxes*, you will pay taxes based on your business's net profit. Because you pay taxes on net profit, what you do with this money after you pay taxes on it has no effect on your taxes. Therefore, if you take all of your remaining net profit as an owner's draw, or none of it, it has no effect on your taxes.

Lots of people find this confusing, and I can understand why; it is confusing. Here's the important point. In a sole proprietorship or single-member LLC, the dollars your business earns in net profit are taxed at the net-profit stage. The business's net profit is considered your money anyway for tax purposes, so it is only taxed once. What happens to the money after that doesn't matter.

To summarize, here are the important points about an owner's draw:

- You do not have to take it (it's already your money).

- You do not pay taxes on it (you pay taxes on net profit, not what you take from the business for personal use).

- It is not a business expense (sorry, since it doesn't go to support your business, you cannot deduct it).

NAIL IT DOWN!

Here are the key elements to remember in managing your books.

Bookkeeping Essentials

❑ Keep your business and personal accounts separate.

❑ A business checking account is the heart of any bookkeeping system; more complex businesses require more elements to track their finances.

❑ Maintain your books regularly.

❑ Keep copies of all records.

❑ Keep your books on the computer only if you are really comfortable doing so. Remember that paper has worked well for thousands of years.

❑ Get expert advice!

Paying Yourself

❑ Sole proprietors and single-member LLC owners will pay themselves through an owner's draw.

❑ The money from an owner's draw comes from net profit, after taxes have been paid.

❑ Because taxes have been paid on net profit, the owner's draw has no effect on taxes.

❑ Owner's draw is optional, and if there is no net profit, there is no draw.

Chapter Fourteen

KNOW ACCOUNTING BASICS

As we mentioned in the last chapter, accounting gives you the tools required to look at the big picture when it comes to your business finances. The accounting process takes all of those daily records you generate in your business and distills them down into three formats that show you how well your business is doing.

In this chapter we'll look at three things:

- Some common but still confusing accounting terms you may hear.

- The three financial statements that are at the heart of accounting.

- What lenders like to see in a business's accounting practices.

Remember, this book can't make you into an accountant. My goal is to make you familiar with the terminology and show you what you need to know to be a smart consumer of accounting services.

ACCOUNTING MYSTERIES REVEALED!

There are a lot of things that many new business owners don't understand about accounting. Accounting is full of its own terminology, and like a patient who doesn't understand the disease he has, having to listen to an accountant use money-related words you don't understand can be confusing. So here is a explanation of three of the most commonly misunderstood accounting ideas: accounts payable and receivable; cash- and accrual-basis accounting; and double-entry bookkeeping.

Accounts Receivable and Payable

Some business owners run their businesses on an all-cash basis. That is, their products or services are paid for when bought, and they in turn pay for their supplies and other expenses when they purchase them. (Buying and selling things "for cash" does not literally mean that dollar bills are exchanged; for accounting purposes checks and credit cards, as well as dollars, usually count as cash.) This is probably the simplest, and best, way to run a business if you can do it. You get paid when you sell something, and you pay for things as you need.

Some industries are commonly run this way. When I take my dog to the veterinarian, I don't get my dog back until I pay for the service.

But many businesses are run, at least some of the time, on a credit basis. This doesn't mean that they use credit cards (which usually gets counted as cash), but rather that the seller extends credit to the purchaser for a certain amount of time. For example, if I do some freelance technical writing, I'll do the work and then send an invoice to my customer, letting them know how much to pay and asking them to send their payment within thirty days.

During those thirty days, I need a way to remember that this money is owed to me. What I would do is set up an account for each customer who owes me money and keep track of each account. When any business sets up an account to keep track of money they are to receive, it is called an Accounts Receivable (AR).

In the same way, your business may purchase some goods through a supplier or business store. You have a good credit history, so they let you pay after thirty days. You'll need a way to remember that you owe this money, so you'll set up an Accounts Payable (AP) for tracking this money that you owe.

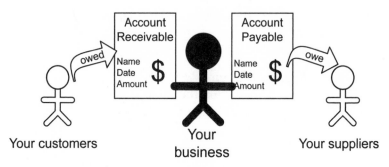

Accounts payable and receivable let you keep track of who owes you money and who you owe money to

The names for these two kinds of accounts are always from your point of view. That is, when you are to receive money, it is an account receivable, and when you are to pay money, it is an account payable.

For many businesses, using AP and AR is a handy way of keeping track of debts owed by and owed to the business. Many experts suggest that if your AR get too old, meaning that those who owe you money are behind on their payment schedule, you should work hard to collect those funds as soon as possible. The older the AR, the more likely they are never to be paid at all.

Cash-Basis vs. Accrual-Basis Accounting
You may wonder when tax time rolls around, do you get to take business tax deductions for the things you have

purchased but haven't yet paid for? What if you buy supplies on terms and payment isn't due until next year? It depends on the accounting method you claim.

The first method is called the cash-basis method. Under this system you consider yourself paid when you actually get paid, and you consider your debts paid when you actually pay them. With the cash-basis system, the transaction always occurs when the cash changes hands. In other words, you would report income in the year you actually got paid for it, and you would report expenses in the year you actually paid them (that is, sent or received the cash or check).

For example, let's say that you bill a client for services in December. The client pays you in January. Do you declare the income for the past year or the next year under the cash-basis system? It would be for the next year, because you didn't get the check until January.

The second method is called the accrual-basis method, and it looks at when you send or receive an invoice for work or purchases. In other words, you would report income in the year you actually earned it and expenses in the year you actually incur them, not when you actually pay them.

For example, let's say that you bill a client for services in December. The client pays you in January. Do you need to declare the income for the past year or the next year under the accrual-basis system? It would be for the past year, because you did the work (and sent the bill) in December.

Why is this important? The IRS requires that you declare one method or the other for tax purposes and then stick with it (you need to justify any change in writing). Most small businesses can use the somewhat simpler cash-basis method, although some businesses will actually keep two sets of books, one for cash basis and the other for accrual. Businesses that maintain large inventories or have large sales may be required to use the accrual method. Talk to your accountant for the best advice.

Single Entry vs. Double Entry

Perhaps you remember in Charles Dickens's *A Christmas Carol*, Bob Cratchit was a bookkeeper working for the miserly Ebenezer Scrooge. Cratchit would sit at his desk all day in a dark, cold office and add up numbers on a ledger. Of course, this was over 100 years ago, and he had no calculator, no computer, just his paper and pen. And he might have been adding up dozens or even hundreds of numbers at a time. So when he got to the end, how would he know if he made a mistake or not? Well, he could do it all again, but what if he got a different answer? Then he'd have to do it a third time; all in all, not a very efficient system. So instead, accountants discovered long ago that there was an efficient system that, while not guaranteeing mistakes couldn't be made, would eliminate most of the errors. The key was in having one system where everything gets counted twice.

The system where you just add everything up just once is called, not surprisingly, single-entry bookkeeping. If you have kept track of your checks in a checkbook, you have done single-entry bookkeeping. You simply add deposits and subtract withdrawals and keep a running total. The main disadvantage to single-entry systems is that if you make a mistake, you might not catch it for a long time, and when you do discover an error it can be difficult to find.

As an example, let's say during a particular month that you had some sales and bought a desk for your home business. When you buy something, you spend cash, so that gets recorded as an expense. The money you receive in exchange for your sales counts as income. So in single-entry bookkeeping you have income and expenses, and the two have nothing to do with each other.

To make bookkeeping more reliable, accountants long ago came up with the notion of double-entry bookkeeping. In double-entry bookkeeping, every transaction is recorded twice, once in each of two balancing categories, as a debit and a credit (and don't bother trying to memorize which is for what). For example, let's say that you purchased a desk for your home office. In double-entry bookkeeping, you record this transaction twice, once because you spent cash on the desk, but also once because the desk has value that increases your assets.

In the same way, when you make sales, you obviously increase your cash, since you take in income. But you also decrease your inventory, since your product goes out the door.

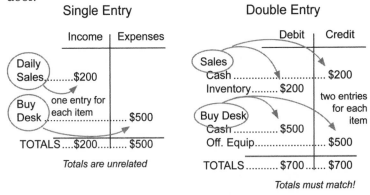

Double-entry bookkeeping adds each transaction twice, once in each of two balancing categories

Every transaction gets recorded in two places like this in double-entry systems, once as a debit and once as a credit. Since everything gets recorded twice, when you add up the debits and credits at the end of the month, they should balance. If they don't, you know instantly that you've made a mistake somewhere along the line. This is the double check that let Bob Cratchit know his math was correct.

No one would expect you to be able to do double-entry bookkeeping based on this brief description. Most small business owners who do their own bookkeeping use the single-entry system because it is easier to understand. In fact, no business owner I know uses double-entry because most find it very confusing. But professional bookkeepers and accountants use double-entry because it is more reliable and can offer insights to your business that single-entry cannot.

FINANCIAL STATEMENTS

How Statements Show the Health of Your Business

Let's say that you are a big sports fan. You really know your team inside and out. A friend of yours, who doesn't know your team that well, asks you how good your team is this year.

You realize that there are several ways to answer this question. "How good" might mean:

- How well they did in their last game, so you might tell your friend the score of the game.

- What their overall record is this season, so you might tell them your team's win-loss record.

- How good the players are, how much depth they have on the bench, for example.

All three of these things, the score, the record, and the depth, all go into explaining how good your team is. Note that all three of these things are related, but they are certainly not identical. The depth of the bench certainly has an effect on how well your team does during the game, which affects the score. And of course the score of the game directly affects the win-loss record. So you really can't get a complete picture of how good your team is without all three, and they all reflect different aspects of the same team.

In the same way, the financial status of your business cannot easily be reflected with one, or even two, types of financial reports. Instead, it will take three different reports, or statements, to show you how well your business is doing. And like the sports example, all three are related, since they all work off of the same business, yet all show a unique view.

The three different statements are:

- Cash flow

- Profit and loss

- Balance sheet

You need to be able to understand and evaluate all three of these statements if you are to have a handle on how financially successful your business is.

Statements vs. Projections

In this discussion, you might wonder what we mean by projections and statements. Sometimes the words get thrown around without being used in their strict sense. Any time that you have a financial record that is a record of what has happened in the past, it is a statement. Any tax records you have, for example, would be statements, since they reflect what happened in a previous year.

But many businesses also want to try and budget for the future, to see what might happen down the road. They would develop financial projections, which are these same financial statements carried into the future. Another term you sometimes see for financial projections is *pro forma*.

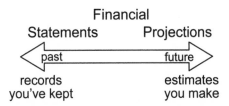

Financial statements are records of business done. Financial projections are estimates of future business.

We'll look in some detail at each of the three financial statements.

CASH FLOW

If you designed a house, you would most likely include a bathtub. Into that bathtub goes water from the spigot, and it goes out again through the drain. You can turn the water on as fast as you want to let water into the tub, and you can open or close the drain to let water out. What two things determine the water level in the tub? First, how fast water pours in, and second, how quickly it drains.

Let's say that your bathtub wasn't set up correctly, so you can never quite stop the water from leaking out of the drain. Furthermore, you like to keep fish, and while you are away on vacation you keep your pet fish in the bathtub.

Say you fill the tub up about halfway for your fish while you are gone for a few days. Because the tub always leaks, you have to leave the spigot open a bit to make sure that enough water is always going in to replace the water leaking out. You watch the water level for a while and it looks like it is steady, so you go on your vacation, leaving the fish with plenty of food.

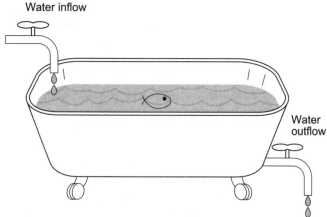

The water level is determined by the rate of water flow in and water flow out

When you return a few days later your fish, unfortunately, has died. You search for the reason why. There was plenty of food, the water temperature was fine, and the level was high enough. What could have gone wrong? (Hint: It's the water level.)

Because the water is constantly flowing in and out, any change in the *rate* of either the water inflow or outflow will affect the level in the tub. While you were away, either the inflow decreased or the outflow increased to the point where the tub drained completely. Then, the situation reversed, so that the tub filled again. In other words, looking at the water level on a periodic basis, such as once a week or month, isn't enough to judge how well your fish will flourish. You need to have plenty of water at all times.

Your business will have a checking account that works a lot like that bathtub. Money will go in and go out, and a challenge that many businesses face is keeping enough cash in the account at all times. It really doesn't matter if you put more money in last week than you needed if you don't have enough this week—you need cash in there at all times.

Cash Flow Is Your Business's Lifeblood

Your business's cash flow works exactly like the water in the tub. Cash goes into your checking account when you make deposits and goes out when you write checks. No cash = no checks = no business. If the tub runs out of water, the fish goes belly-up. If your business runs out of cash, it is probably doomed as well.

Cash flow means keeping track of your cash inflows and outflows day by day, so that you never run out. There are two significant differences between your bathtub and your checkbook, though. First, there is an upper limit on how much water you can put in your tub without it spilling over, but there is no limit on how much money you can have in your checking account. Second, there is a limit on how little water you can have in your tub. When it is empty, you're dry. But there is no such limit on how much you spend out of your checking account. There is nothing to stop you from writing a check for $1,000 even if you only have $10 in your checking account. Of course, the overdraft will catch up with you eventually, but it might be better to think of your checking account more like your bathtub—when it is empty the checks must stop.

Cash flow is especially important in small businesses because cash is the lifeblood of your business, and if you don't have any blood, you're dead. Just as putting water in the tub after you get out of the bath doesn't get you clean, having money on hand after you owe it doesn't get business done. You have to have adequate cash at all times, not just at the end of the month or end of the year. Timing is essential to maintaining a positive cash flow.

Managing Cash Flow

Just as there are three ways to increase the water level in your tub (increasing the rate of the water going in, slowing the rate of water going out, or adding water from an outside source), there are three ways to improve your cash flow:

- Increase the rate of cash coming into the business. If you bill customers on a regular basis, try to find ways to get your money faster. You won't make any more money in the long run, but you will improve your cash flow. Also, don't ignore overdue payments. Call and ask the customer what is wrong and offer to set up a payment schedule. Some of your customers may be having cash flow problems themselves and will only pay creditors who aggressively seek payment. Be one of those creditors.

- Slow the rate of cash going out of the business. If you have bills to pay on a regular basis, see if you can pay them less often (this is exactly the opposite of the previous strategy). Don't pay bills until they are due. If an invoice gives you thirty or forty-five days to pay, take advantage of the time and don't write the check until shortly before the invoice is due. If you take a draw, don't take it until you can see that you will have enough money for the month. If you know you are going to face increases in expenses, try to get more income during those periods as well.

- If your cash flow is poor but you are profitable, you might be able to inject some additional capital into the business. Sometimes you just need some money to get you over a hump and then you should be OK, so if you have some personal savings, you can always put that into the business. Or you might be able to go to a bank for a line of credit. But one word of caution: If you go to a bank, be prepared to show them a statement showing your current cash flow and how your future business will overcome any problems in the future.

Just as you have no one to blame except yourself if your tub runs out of water, your business's cash flow is your responsibility. Each is a matter of knowing how much is going in and out, and planning to make sure that enough is always available. Cash flow is a management issue, and to be successful you will have to manage your cash flow or it will manage you. It doesn't really matter if your business is profitable or not at the end of the month because if you can't pay your bills in the middle of the month, you are out of business. But by planning for when the money comes in and goes out, you can manage your cash flow and not only make a profit but maintain a positive cash flow as well.

Also note that the way to improve cash-flow is not necessarily by working harder! You may not need more income if your cash flow is poor, you may just need to speed the rate at which the money you are already earning comes in and slow the rate of your expenses going out. In many cases, business owners find they make enough money, they just don't manage the cash flow to keep the fish swimming.

Shown below is a simple example of a monthly cash-flow projection. Note that although this projection is on a monthly basis, you could just as easily create a projection based on daily cash flow.

Cash Flow Example

Month	April	May	June	July	Aug	Sept
Beginning Cash Balance	$7,000	$5,550	$6,360	$7,260	$8,040	$9,340
Cash Inflows (Income):						
Sales & Receipts	$3,750	$4,000	$4,500	$4,500	$4,500	$4,500
Total Cash Inflows	$3,750	$4,000	$4,500	$4,500	$4,500	$4,500
Cash Outflows (Expenses):						
Advertising	$500	$240	$240	$200	$120	$100
Insurance	$250			$250		
Inventory Purchases	$1,000	$500	$500	$600	$600	$600
Permits & Licenses	$100					
Professional Fees	$500			$200		
Rent or Lease	$1,200	$1,200	$1,200	$1,200	$1,200	$1,200
Telephone	$250	$100	$100	$100	$100	$100
Utilities	$150	$150	$160	$170	$180	$190
Estimated Taxes	$250		$400			$500
Owner's Draw	$1,000	$1,000	$1,000	$1,000	$1,000	$1,000
Total Cash Outflows	$5,200	$3,190	$3,600	$3,720	$3,200	$3,690
Ending Cash Balance	$5,550	$6,360	$7,260	$8,040	$9,340	$10,150

All cash inflows and outflows are tracked in your cash flow. It looks a lot like your checkbook register.

Note that the ending cash balance for one month becomes the beginning cash balance the next month. Cash flow is continuous.

This business is doing well by maintaining a positive cash flow.

PROFIT AND LOSS

Does your business make money? To see, you'll have to look at your profit and loss statement. A profit and loss statement provides a summary of how much money came into the business versus how much went out over a given period of time.

Profit and loss statements go by different names, such as revenue and expense, or income statements. Actually, revenue and expense is probably the most descriptive name because that is what the statement shows. The profit or loss is only the periodic total of all of the revenue (income) of the business minus the expenses over a period of time. We'll call it the P&L in this chapter.

Remember how we calculated the net profit your business made? We looked at how income flowed through cost of goods sold to give gross profit, and gross profit flowed through other expenses to give the net profit. Here is another way of showing the same thing:

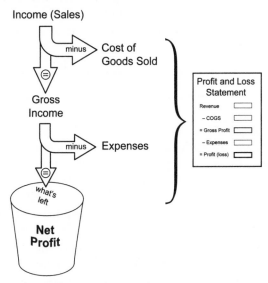

A profit and loss statement provides a periodic summary of the money coming into and going out of the business, with the final result in the net-profit (or loss) bucket

Let's say that you tracked all of your income and expenses on a daily basis but only added them up and looked in your net-profit bucket at the end of the month. You would add up your income (money that you earned selling your product), your cost of goods (money you spent to buy and create your product), and other business expenses. Whatever was left in the bucket was your net profit. You would have a loss if you earned less than you spent. Losses are usually indicated either in negative numbers such as -100 or are put in parentheses (100) or may be colored red (thus being "in the red" means losing money and "in the black" means profitable).

This flow of funds is what a profit and loss statement shows. A P&L provides a summary of the activity of the business over a certain period, usually a month, quarter, or year.

The P&L is different from a cash flow in two ways. First, a cash flow is concerned only with cash, whereas a P&L is concerned with all sources of income and expense, even those that are not cash-flow items. For example, owner's draw is a cash-flow item but not a P&L item because only monies you spend to directly support your business are considered expenses. On the other hand, new (unpaid) accounts payable and receivable could be considered P&L items but would never be a cash-flow item because no cash has actually changed hands.

Second, recall that your cash flow looks at the ups and downs of your cash on a continuous basis—how high is the water in the tub right now? But a P&L is only concerned with the level at the end of a period of time, say a quarter. If you happen to measure your P&L only at times when your cash is up, you might mistakenly believe that all was well, when in fact your cash flow was poor in between (remember the poor fish!).

Profit and loss statements, as shown on the next page, look a lot like cash-flow statements and share many of the same categories because both deal with money going into and out of the business. But remember a cash flow deals only with cash, whereas a P&L shows all forms of income and expense. So a P&L will show cost of goods as a category, for example.

The other significant difference is that each time period on a P&L is separate from all of the others. Recall that in a cash flow the ending balance of one period becomes the starting balance for the next period. But in a P&L, each period starts fresh.

Profit and Loss Example

Month	April	May	June	July	Aug	Sept
Revenue:						
Cash Sales	$3,750	$4,000	$4,500	$4,500	$4,500	$4,500
Credit Sales						
Other						
Net Sales	$3,750	$4,000	$4,500	$4,500	$4,500	$4,500
Cost of Goods Sold:						
Material	$800	$500	$500	$600	$600	$600
Labor						
Cost of Goods Sold	$800	$500	$500	$600	$600	$600
Gross Profit (Loss)	$2,950	$3,500	$4,000	$3,900	$3,900	$3,900
Expenses:						
Advertising	$500	$240	$240	$200	$120	$100
Depreciation	$100	$100	$100	$100	$100	$100
Insurance	$250			$250		
Permits and Licenses	$100					
Professional Fees	$500			$200		
Rent or Lease	$1,200	$1,200	$1,200	$1,200	$1,200	$1,200
Telephone	$200	$100	$100	$80	$80	$80
Utilities	$150	$150	$160	$170	$180	$190
Total Expenses	$3,000	$1,790	$1,800	$2,200	$1,680	$1,670
Net Income (Loss)	($50)	$1,710	$2,200	$1,700	$2,220	$2,230

Note that all sources of income and expense are typically shown on a P&L, but cash-only outflows, such as an owner s draw, are not.

Unlike a cash flow, the P&L looks at each month individually. Manageable losses in early months are quite common.

This business is turning a small profit every month. How can we tell where this money is going? The balance sheet will give us a clue.

BALANCE SHEET

So far we have looked at two of the financial statements, a cash-flow statement and a profit and loss statement. The third, no less important, is the balance sheet. Of the three financial statements, the balance sheet presents the broadest picture of your business. It looks at everything your business owns and owes, and provides an overview of the health of your business.

Unlike your cash flow, which looks at money continuously, and the P&L, which looks at money on a periodic basis, the balance sheet looks at where your money is at one instant. It is like a snapshot of your business health, kind of like an X-ray. If we did a balance sheet today and another one tomorrow, they would probably be a little different because the business changes. There will be larger changes month to month and year to year, and hopefully the balance sheet will show your business getting healthier as time goes by.

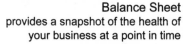

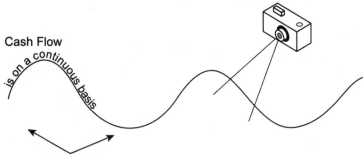

Balance Sheet
provides a snapshot of the health of your business at a point in time

Cash Flow
is on a continuous basis

Profit and Loss
provides a summary of financial activity on a periodic basis

Each of the financial statements look at your business finances in a unique way

The balance sheet looks at three things: assets, liabilities, and net worth (also called equity).

An asset is anything that the business owns. This might be equipment, supplies, office furniture, cash, whatever. If the business owns it and it has value, it is an asset.

A liability is any debt the business has or anything the business owes. Loans and accounts payable are probably the most common business debts.

The difference between what you own (asset) and what you owe (liability) is your net worth, or equity. The formula for calculating the equity is:

Assets – Liabilities = Equity, or
A – L = E

To take a simple example, let's say you buy a car that is valued at $10,000. You paid $4,000 in cash for the car but took out a loan for the remaining $6,000. What is the asset, liability, and equity?

Car	= $10,000	=	Asset (own)
Loan	= $6,000	=	Liability (owe)
Cash	= $4,000	=	Equity (your investment)

Ignoring any depreciation, the asset is $10,000 (what the car is worth) and the liability is the $6,000 loan (what you owe). Your equity in the car is what you put into it, $4,000 (your investment). Put into the equity formula, this would look like:

Assets	–	Liabilities	=	Equity
$10,000	–	$6,000	=	$4,000

Another way of looking at this is to think about what the business has and who paid for it. Typically what a business owns is stuff. That stuff might be in the form of equipment, cash, or furniture as we mentioned before. But that stuff has value. Assets are stuff.

Your liabilities and equity represent who has paid for the stuff in the business. If you have a loan, then someone else paid for the stuff that the loan money purchased. On the other hand, if you bought the business furniture with your cash, then you own it, so you have equity in the furniture.

Based on the car example above, the car is the stuff, so the asset is $10,000. Who paid for the stuff? The bank paid $6,000 (liability), and you paid $4,000 (equity).

A balance sheet is called a balance sheet because when it is arranged correctly, the two sides balance. One side is always assets (stuff) and the other side is always liabilities and equity (who paid what for the stuff). If the two sides don't balance, then something is wrong. For the car example, the asset ($10,000) equals the liability ($6,000) plus the equity ($4,000).

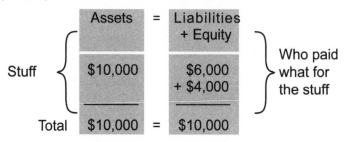

Balance Sheet Example

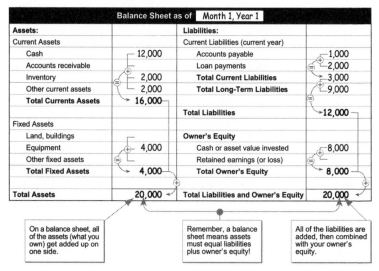

Balance Sheet as of	Month 1, Year 1		
Assets:		**Liabilities:**	
Current Assets		Current Liabilities (current year)	
Cash	12,000	Accounts payable	1,000
Accounts receivable		Loan payments	2,000
Inventory	2,000	**Total Current Liabilities**	3,000
Other current assets	2,000	**Total Long-Term Liabilities**	9,000
Total Currents Assets	16,000		
		Total Liabilities	12,000
Fixed Assets			
Land, buildings		**Owner's Equity**	
Equipment	4,000	Cash or asset value invested	8,000
Other fixed assets		Retained earnings (or loss)	
Total Fixed Assets	4,000	**Total Owner's Equity**	8,000
Total Assets	20,000	**Total Liabilities and Owner's Equity**	20,000

On a balance sheet, all of the assets (what you own) get added up on one side.

Remember, a balance sheet means assets must equal liabilities plus owner's equity!

All of the liabilities are added, then combined with your owner's equity.

Reading a Balance Sheet

By looking at the relationship of your assets, liabilities, and equity and how these values change over time, an observer can get a good idea of how healthy your business is. They tell the reader how much debt your business has taken on and how much it has in equity. Debt is not always a bad thing, but like a hole, if it is too deep, you may never get out.

Balance sheets can be hard to decipher until you get used to them. Sometimes they put assets on one side and liabilities and equity on the other (like the example here), sometimes they put everything in one column. In either case, you'll generally see both short-term and long-term categories for both assets and liabilities. "Short term," "current," or "liquid" means an asset can be converted to cash or that a liability is due in less than one year. "Long term" or "fixed" means an asset will be converted to cash in more than a year or that a liability is due in more than year.

When reading a balance sheet, look carefully to see how the numbers add up—sometimes it isn't obvious which numbers come from where. Pay attention to the rows marked Total.

Because balance sheets are current for only one day, each must be labeled for the day it was created.

What Lenders Look for in Financials

If you put together a business plan for a bank or other lender, they will want to see either actual financial statements from your business or projections you have made (recall that *pro forma* is another term for financial projections). You may wonder how you can know how much money you will have if you haven't done any business yet. This is a problem, but you should be able to make educated guesses based on your market research. What exactly will a banker look for in these projections?

Cash Flow

Bankers like to see a monthly cash flow projection for the first year of business and usually quarterly projections for years two and three. Cash flow is one of the most important ways a lender has of deciding whether or not you can pay them back. Although you may have collateral and good credit, these by themselves do not pay loans back; cash does, and you need cash flow to generate it.

Profit and Loss

Lenders often will want to see profit and loss statements for the first three or five years, usually month by month for the first year, quarterly for the next one or two, and then yearly for the next years. This doesn't mean that a lender will expect you to be profitable in the first year, or even two. But they will want to see if you have the resources to keep your business going if you aren't yet profitable and how you will build your business to the point of profitability.

Balance Sheet

Finally, a banker will want to see balance sheet projections that show an increase in equity over time. This shows that you are reinvesting profits in your business rather than spending them on personal items. Plus, bankers like to see that you have made a personal investment in your business by putting some of your personal equity into the business. No lender wants to risk its money on a business that the owner isn't willing to risk his or her own money on.

Ideally your business will show an asset to liability ratio of at least 2:1, meaning your assets are twice your liabilities. This will help ensure that you can weather tough times without having a negative net worth.

All of your projections should be consistent; that is, did you use the same numbers to generate the forms or did you just make them up? The best place to start is in your cash-flow projections, which will generate your profit and loss, both of which are required for your balance sheet. It is clear to anyone with experience if you make up numbers. For example, if you run a gift shop and show the same profit and loss all twelve months, the lender will know that you haven't done your homework because gift shops do most of their business in December and much less during other months. And if your cash flow is poor but you show a profit each month, the lender will wonder where the additional money is coming from.

For more information on how to create financial projections for your business, see chapter 16, *Know How To Write A Business Plan.*

NAIL IT DOWN!

Here are the key elements to understanding accounting basics and financial statements.

Accounting Basics

❑ Accounts payable and receivable give you a way to track who you owe money to and who owes you money.

❑ Using a cash-basis accounting system means you count income when you actually get paid and expenses when you actually pay them.

❑ Using the accrual accounting system means you count income when you earn it (send the invoice) and expenses when you incur them (receive the bill or invoice).

❑ Single-entry bookkeeping records each transaction once; double entry counts each transaction twice, once in each of two balancing categories. Nearly all small business owners use single entry.

Financial Statements

❑ Cash flow shows how cash comes into and goes out of your business on a continuous basis.

❑ A profit and loss statement provides a summary of the financial activity in the business over a period of time.

❑ A balance sheet provides a snapshot of the health of your business at a point in time by looking at your assets, liabilities, and net worth or equity.

❑ Of the different financial statements, a positive cash flow is the most essential to a young business, because cash is the lifeblood of the business.

Chapter Fifteen

Know How to Minimize Your Taxes

How to Cut Your Taxes to Zero

L et's face it—nobody likes paying taxes. It seems like such a waste that you work so hard to earn this money and then you have to fork over some of it to the government.

Actually, it is easy, and legal, not to pay any taxes. Since the amount you pay in taxes is based on your net profit, that is, your income after you have subtracted all costs and expenses, you simply have to make sure you have no net profit. Put into the simplest possible terms, just make sure you don't make any money. No profit = no taxes. Of course, this will also mean no groceries, no clothes, no rent. But hey! You got out of paying taxes!

In this chapter we'll get an overview of the kinds of taxes many businesses have to pay, what goes into a tax return, and how to use deductions to keep your taxes down. This chapter will definitely not make you a tax expert. Rather, it is designed to give an understanding of how business taxes work, so that you can get appropriate advice and keep your taxes as low as legally possible.

Taxes Are a Good Problem

Taxes are a good problem to have. If you are making enough money to pay taxes, you are making some real money. Ask yourself, would you rather pay 35 percent in taxes on $100,000 income or 0 percent of $10,000? I'll take the higher taxes every time.

Plus, you wouldn't expect to go to a ball game without paying for a ticket or to ride on a bus without handing over your fare. In the same way, you can look at paying taxes as the admission to the most fair and most stable economy in the world, and your fare to hop on the most sophisticated and dynamic game available. The government, financial system, and public institutions that make the economy run are like everything else—they cost money to maintain, and your taxes are your admission.

THREE KEY WORDS (AGAIN!)

Get Expert Advice

As we'll see, taxes for a small, one-person sole proprietor or LLC are relatively straightforward. But for most other businesses, with several employees, partners, or a significant inventory, taxes quickly become a mess. The easiest solution to this problem is to get expert advice.

TAXPAYER PREREQUISITES

Before you even think about paying your business taxes, you need to consider some preliminary steps that may be required. In this section we'll look at some of the things you should do before you even make that first sale.

Have a Bookkeeping System

We've already talked about money management and having a bookkeeping system set up. Making sure that you have a separate business checking account, for example, and keeping your books up to date will make preparing your taxes much easier and less expensive than trying to catch up at the end of the year.

Part of managing your money effectively is knowing what records to keep and for how long. We'll address these issues in more detail later.

Get an Employer Identification Number (EIN)

Just as the government uses your Social Security number to identify you as an individual for tax purposes, the IRS also has numbers to identify businesses for tax purposes. These numbers are employer identification numbers. Despite their name, EINs can be used by any business, not just those with employees.

Sometimes you'll hear these numbers referred to as tax identification numbers, or TINs. While this name is frequently used and means the same thing, the correct term is employer identification number.

The IRS requires an EIN for all corporations and LLCs as well, and they are also required for any business with employees.

EINs are optional for sole proprietors without employees, but even these businesses may be requested by others to have one. Why? As we discussed earlier, some unethical businesses attempt to avoid paying taxes by claiming that they, or their workers, are independent contractors rather than employees. Since having an EIN indicates that a business is truly in business, those you do business with, such as suppliers, banks, or businesses hiring you, may request your EIN for their records.

So, if you are not a sole proprietor, you'll have to get an EIN, and if you are, you may have to get one anyway. Don't hesitate to get one—they're free and easy to get.

How to Get One

Obtaining an EIN is probably the easiest thing you'll do to start your business. First, get a free copy of IRS Form SS-4 (all IRS forms and publications are free and available online at http://www.irs.gov). This form will give you some background information and let you collect the information the IRS needs. Then you'll need to contact the IRS either by mail, fax, phone, or online to give the IRS the information it needs.

FEDERAL TAXES YOU WILL OWE

When you work for someone else as an employee, the employer is responsible for withholding a part of your wages. This payroll tax is withheld from every paycheck because the government knows that if they left it up to the individual employees to pay their own taxes, many of them wouldn't, and then everyone would be unhappy.

But when you are self-employed, there is no employer to withhold your taxes for you. Now you are responsible for setting aside and paying your own taxes, and it is a responsibility that you should take seriously. Not only is it the right thing to do, but you can get into some pretty serious trouble if you don't. In this section we'll look at what those taxes are, and how you pay them.

Estimated Taxes

Four times a year the IRS requires you to file estimated taxes, assuming your business meets the conditions to do so. Not everyone who is self-employed has to file estimated taxes, but many do. According to the IRS, estimated taxes must be filed by anyone:

- Who does not have taxes withheld by someone else (such as an employer), and

- Expects to owe $1,000 in taxes.

The first criteria means that you are not working for someone else who might withhold taxes for you. This means that if you are both an employee and self-employed, you may be able to use your payroll taxes to offset what you would otherwise pay in estimated taxes.

The second criteria simply means that if you expect your total taxes due for the year to be less than $1,000, you do not need to file quarterly.

Estimated Taxes Gotchas!
Be careful with estimated taxes! Because you are supposed to file estimated taxes quarterly, you can get into trouble if you don't file in the quarter that you received your income. For example, if you made enough money to owe estimated taxes in Quarter 1 but didn't pay for that quarter, then did pay later in the year, you may owe a penalty even though your total taxes paid for the year was correct.

Filing Estimated Taxes
Filing estimated taxes can be scary for the first year because you aren't sure how much you need to send in. Here are three things to keep in mind.

First, you don't have to worry too much if you don't send enough in the first year because of the "safe harbor" rules we'll discuss next.

Second, you will have a much better idea after the first year how much you really owe based on how much additional tax you owe or the refund you receive at the end of the year.

Finally, a good rule of thumb is to simply set aside about 20 percent of your net profit in any quarter and send that in as your estimated taxes to the IRS. Note that if your state has an income tax, you should probably set aside another 5 percent for them and be sure to send that in to your state taxing authority as well.

You file your estimated taxes using Form 1040-ES, available from the IRS. Once the IRS receives your initial estimated tax payment, they'll send you envelopes and vouchers for future payments so that all you have to do is write the check and put a stamp on the envelope.

Safe Harbor Rules
You will not be charged a penalty if the estimated taxes you pay totals either:

- 90 percent of the taxes you owe that year, or

- 100 percent of the taxes you owed last year.

These limits, called the "safe harbor" rules, make it fairly easy to avoid a penalty for your first year or two in business. You won't be penalized as long as your tax payments this year were at least as much as the previous year. If your income goes up from year to year, the 100 percent rule will keep you safe. For example, if your taxes the previous year were $1,000 and you made estimated payments this year of at least $1,000, you would not be charged a penalty even if you owe more than $1,000 this year. Of course, you still owe the taxes due.

Just like with regular income taxes, if you overpay during the year, you can choose to receive a refund.

When Estimated Taxes Are Due
Estimated tax payments are due four times per year. Notice that although the dates are spread out, they are not all three months apart:

- April 15

  For the first payment of the year. This is the same date as your regular 1040 for the previous year, and if you file your return early you can apply any refund for the previous year to this year's first estimated payment.

- June 15

- September 15

- January 15

  For the final payment of the previous year.

Your estimated tax payments go towards covering several different federal taxes you owe, including income tax and self-employment tax.

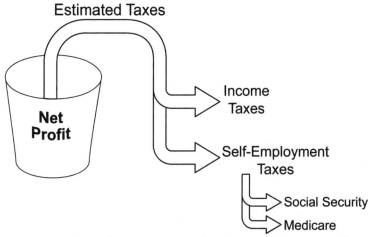

Your estimated taxes go toward paying your income and self-employment taxes

Income Tax

First, estimated taxes go toward paying your income tax. This is simply the tax you owe based on your income, and it goes to support general government operations. This is the same tax you would pay if you were employed by someone else. The percentage you owe increases as your income goes up, from 0 percent for low-income earners to 35 percent for those earning well over $300,000. Most will pay in the neighborhood of 25 percent federal income tax.

Self-Employment Tax

Self-employment taxes are separate from income, taxes and they go towards paying your Social Security and Medicare taxes.

When you work as an employee, the government takes 7.65 percent of your wages for combined Social Security and Medicare (6.2 percent for Social Security and 1.45 percent for Medicare). Your employer also chips in an additional 7.65 percent for a total of 15.3 percent.

When you are self-employed, the entire 15.3 percent tax liability falls on you. In other words, you are paying more in taxes to be self-employed than you would to be employed by someone else. (To be fair, you do get a small amount of this back in what is called the self-employment deduction.)

Who Owes Self-Employment Taxes

It turns out that the threshold for paying your self-employment taxes is different than for your income taxes. In fact, it is much lower, so it is quite possible that you will owe $0 in income taxes yet still have to pay self-employment taxes. You only have to have a net profit of about $433 to owe self-employment taxes.

The moral here is that you should fill out and file your Schedule C (Net Profit From Business) and SE (Self-Employment Tax) even if you make little or no money on your business. Even if your business has a loss and you owe no taxes of any kind, you'll come out ahead because you might be able to offset other taxes you owe this year or next.

For More Information on Estimated and Self-Employment Taxes

❑ IRS publication 505, Tax Withholding and Estimated Taxes

❑ IRS Form 1040-ES, Estimated Taxes for Individuals

❑ IRS Schedule SE, Self Employment Taxes

OTHER TAXES

In addition to federal and state income taxes and your Social Security and Medicare taxes paid through your self-employment taxes, you may be responsible for collecting and paying other taxes as well. Two of these would be payroll taxes, which are collected and paid on behalf of any employees you have, and sales taxes.

Payroll Taxes

If you have employees, you will be required to calculate the amount of money that they owe for income and payroll taxes, as well as your contribution, and remit those amounts to the IRS and your state regularly. There are about twenty-five different laws that cover payroll taxes, and following all of these laws can be quite cumbersome.

Rather than try to explain this complicated topic here, here's a suggestion: Don't handle the payroll taxes yourself. Many business owners find it extremely frustrating and time consuming.

Instead, either talk to your bookkeeper or accountant to see how much he or she would charge you to take on this responsibility. Alternatively, there are lots of companies that handle this for all sizes of businesses. Rather than you calculating the taxes, writing the checks, and sending the money to the IRS, you simply write a check to the payroll company and it does all the work.

Fees charged by payroll companies are not unreasonable, and I've had many business owners tell me they wouldn't think of not using a payroll service. You'll find them listed in your local Yellow Pages.

For More Information on Payroll Taxes

❑ See IRS Publication 15, Employer's Tax Guide

State Sales Taxes

Most states require businesses doing business within their borders to collect and reimburse state sales taxes. Although the rules will vary somewhat from state to state, I will cover the basics here and leave it to you to discover the details where you live and do business.

How Sales Taxes Work

Unlike your income or self-employment taxes, you as a business do not technically pay sales taxes on the goods that you sell. Rather, you collect these taxes from your customers and then reimburse these funds to your state on a regular basis. In other words, this money is never yours. You are simply collecting and holding it on the state's behalf. It is the final consumer of a product that is responsible for these taxes.

For example, let's say that you sell your product for $100. In most counties of my state, that would result in a total sale of $105.55–$100 for me, $5.50 collected in state sales tax, and $.05 in county sales tax. I would hold onto the $5.55 until the end of the quarter when I would send the state 5.5 percent of my total sales for that period.

How Businesses Get in Trouble with Sales Taxes

You would be surprised at how many businesses get into trouble because they can't pay their sales taxes when they are supposed to. They collect the sales taxes properly, put them in the bank, and then fail to hold onto them. Instead, they use the "free money" to buy other materials and equipment, or maybe just splurge on a new personal boat. As a result, at the end of the quarter or other period when they have to send the money to the state, they come up short. This starts a spiral of decline that ends up seeing many businesses in bankruptcy.

This is one reason many states enforce their sales tax laws so strictly. They know that many businesses don't manage their funds well. Most states have significant penalties for failure to pay sales taxes on time, even if the amount of money involved is small.

Collecting Sales Taxes

Before you begin your business in earnest, you should check with your state's taxing authority about obtaining a seller's permit. Seller's permits are the license that allows you to make sales and collect sales taxes and are required in most states. Your local governments may also have regulations covering sales, so check with them as well.

After you have your selle r's permit, you may also want to get a tax-exemption certificate. Because only the final consumer of a product needs to pay the sales taxes, you as the manufacturer or wholesaler do not need to pay sales taxes on the goods that you buy to resell. So if you buy lumber, nails, and glue, for instance, to make into birdhouses that you sell, you don't have to pay sales taxes on these materials that you purchase. Once you have obtained a tax-exempt number, you can show it to the supplier where you purchase your materials and they will not charge you sales tax. However, if you purchase things you will use in your business that are not for resale, such as office equipment, you will have to pay sales taxes on these items (although they are deductible business expenses, and we'll talk about these in more detail later).

Keep in mind also that generally you have to collect sales taxes for whichever state you do business in. This means that if you do business outside of your home state, you need to obtain a seller's permit and collect sales taxes for whatever state you are in when you make sales. For example, if you are an artist and travel in your region to art shows outside of your home state, you will probably have to collect sales taxes in the state where the show is located.

Use Taxes

States that collect sales taxes realize that not all items that customers purchase within the state come from within that state. For example, that computer you purchase to help you track your business finances may be bought through the Internet from a company in another state. Since that business isn't in your state, they generally won't collect sales taxes for your state. But, you are still responsible for paying the tax.

That's right, even though the business doesn't collect the sales tax, you are still responsible for paying it. Now it is called use tax, because you are using the product within your state.

Many people have never heard of the use tax and haven't been paying it because its existence hasn't been well publicized. Be aware that you may be responsible for it.

For More Information on Sales Taxes

❑ http://www.taxadmin.org/fta/link/forms.html

This website from the Federation of Tax Administrators has links to each state's online tax websites.

❑ http://www.taxes.ca/info/index.php

This website has all the links you'll need for Canadian tax information.

❑ Contact your state and local taxing authorities.

How Your Tax Return Works

If you haven't filled out a tax return for your business yet, you'll probably find the process confusing. Not only do you have to file your individual tax return, but now you'll have lots more information to keep track of and more forms to fill out. (Sounds like some good reasons to get expert help!) In this section I'll describe the basic process for filling out your business tax return. We won't go into too much detail, just enough so that you know what each form is for and the process used to calculate your tax due.

But first, this caution. This outline of a tax return applies only to the most basic of businesses, such as a sole proprietor or a single-member LLC with no employees. The reason we can't go into more detail is simple—to do so would require a complete book unto itself. So, if you are running a solo business, feel free to follow along. If your business is more complicated, you know what to do!

Do I Have to File a Return?

In a word, yes, you should. If your business makes a net profit, you are required to pay taxes, and to calculate the correct amount owed, you have to complete and file the forms we'll discuss.

But, even if your business has a loss, it is usually in your interest to file a return for two reasons. First, if your business has a loss you may be able to use this to offset any other income you had for the year. For example, if your business is just getting started part-time, and you had another job, you paid taxes on your personal income. But you can use your business loss to offset the personal income and thus pay less in income taxes.

Second, you might be able to carry over the business loss to future years when you will have a profit and thus lower your taxes in the future. Consult with your accountant on how to make this option work.

You might wonder if you actually have to turn a profit with your business. The answer is, eventually yes. Because in the past some people established shell businesses with the sole purpose of losing money to offset income in other areas, the IRS generally requires that all businesses make a profit every three out of five years. In other words, if you are just getting started, you have three years to make a profit. This shouldn't be a difficult goal. Who wants to start a business that won't make money for three years?

Forms You'll Need

Small solo businesses will generally use three forms for calculating and reporting their taxes: Schedule C, Schedule SE, and Form 1040. Partnerships and corporations will have additional forms. Try to follow along with the diagram on page 207 as we discuss how these forms are used.

Schedule C

Schedule C is where your business reports its income and expenses and calculates the resulting. In fact, most of the figures you will use on Schedule C will come directly from your P&L statement.

Schedule C starts out by asking for your gross receipts, or sales (also called gross sales or revenue). You then subtract your cost of goods sold, which is why you have to track your inventory throughout the year. (If you run a service business and do not sell goods, you have no cost of goods and can ignore this.) Subtracting cost of goods from gross income gives gross profit (this formula should sound familiar by now).

Once you know your gross profit, you can subtract your business expenses. These are all of the famous business deductions that you hear so much about, which we'll discuss in detail shortly.

What's left at the end is your net profit. This figure will get carried over to your Schedule SE (for calculating self-employment tax due) and Form 1040 (for calculating income tax due). If you lose money, you'll have a net loss.

Schedule SE

Schedule SE is where you calculate the amount of self-employment tax due. Remember, your self-employment taxes are your Social Security and Medicare taxes, and you'll pay more for these taxes being self-employed than you would as an employee.

There are short and long versions of the Schedule SE, depending on the nature of your business. Some very simple businesses can use the short version; most will use the long version.

Your self-employment tax calculation starts off with the net profit calculation you completed on Schedule C. Then

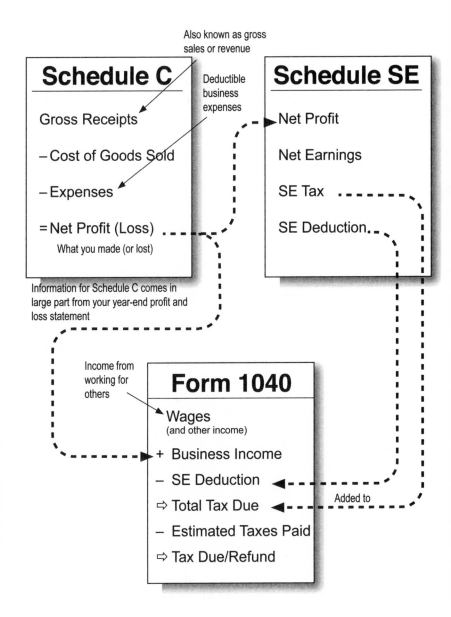

you'll multiply this by a factor to calculate what is called net earnings. This is done to see if you have to pay self-employment tax. If your net earnings are less than $400, you do not owe self-employment taxes. Note that this is a very low threshold; in other words, almost everyone with a profit from self-employment income will owe self-employment tax. The amount due is also carried over to your Form 1040 and adds to your total tax due.

Next you'll calculate your self-employment tax due. Then you'll multiply this amount by 50 percent to get a number for a self-employment tax deduction. Don't be fooled into thinking you get 50 percent of the tax back—you don't. You'll end up getting about 10 percent back, but this is the way they calculate it. This figure is also carried over to your Form 1040 for the actual deduction calculation.

Form 1040

Everyone who files a tax return will complete a Form 1040 or one of its variations (such as Form 1040EZ). The 1040 is the main form, where all of the detailed information derived on other forms is carried over to. It is the mother of all forms, so to speak. For this discussion, we'll discuss only how your business income works into your Form 1040.

To calculate your income taxes due, you are required to report all sources of income on your Form 1040. For most of us these sources would include wages, and some will have interest income, perhaps dividends, or unemployment compensation. These may require their own forms. You'll report your self-employment income on the line called Business Income, and you will have to attach Schedule C.

Next you can calculate certain adjustments to income in the form of deductions (these are separate from business deductions, which were calculated on your Schedule C). This is where you report the one-half of self-employment tax you calculated on Schedule SE. The result at the end of page one of your Form 1040 is your adjusted gross income.

Then you get to calculate your income taxes due, starting with your adjusted gross income and taking into account certain personal deductions. In the section called Other Taxes, you report your self-employment tax due, as calculated on Schedule SE, and this gets added to your other taxes for a total tax due.

If you have made estimated tax payments or had taxes withheld from wages, you should have already paid in most of your taxes due. Enter the amount you have paid in and the amount due to calculate if you have overpaid and are due a refund or have underpaid and owe more.

If you have overpaid and are due a refund, you can choose to apply some or all of your overpayment to next year's estimated tax payments. This is up to you. If you are filing near April 15, when your first estimated tax payment is due, you might consider just letting the IRS keep it. However, if you are filing early, especially if the amount of money is substantial, consider getting the money back. It can earn interest for you instead of for the IRS, and it will improve your cash flow.

For More Information on Small Business Taxes

❏ See IRS Publication 334, Tax Guide for Small Business

REDUCING YOUR TAXES (LEGALLY!)

Q. Who is legally responsible for calculating how much you and your business owe in taxes?

A. You.

You are responsible for your taxes. The government collects them and gets upset if you make a mistake, but it is you who does the figuring. Of course, you don't want to pay too much because that would be a waste, and you don't want to pay too little because then you are looking at penalties. So how can you legally pay as little as possible?

Besides the simplistic answer of not making any money, one secret is to does what you can to keep your bottom line as low as possible. You can do this through taking deductions for legitimate business expenses.

Common Business Deductions

Remember when we talked about your income and expenses and we said that your net profit was calculated from this formula:

> Gross Income – Cost of Goods Sold =
> Gross Profit – Expenses = Net Profit, or
> GI – COGS = GP – Ex = NP

Since you pay taxes based on your net profit, you can see by the formula that any dollars you spend on your cost of goods sold will not be taxed. In the same way, if you have business expenses, these dollars come off the bottom line and will also not be taxed. This means you can legally deduct from your taxes any ordinary and necessary business expense.

The key is the term "ordinary and necessary." As we'll see, nearly all common business expenses can be taken as deductions, and chances are there are some you have never thought of. As one CPA put it, "If you spend a buck to make a buck, it's probably deductible."

A Common Misunderstanding

Before we proceed, let me clear up one common misunderstanding that can cost you. That is that your expenses are essentially free if you take them as business deductions. No! Taking a business deduction for an item you buy does save you taxes compared to buying it without the deduction, but it is in no way free. The deduction you get is equivalent to the tax bracket you are in.

Here's an example. Let's say that you buy a computer printer for personal use for $100. Since you pay for the printer with the taxable wages you earn, you will pay income taxes on the $100 you spend to buy the printer, depending on your income tax bracket. But if you buy that printer for your business, the $100 can be a deductible business expense, which means your business will pay zero dollars in taxes on that $100. You might save anywhere from ten to thirty-five dollars or more in taxes, depending on your tax bracket.

So, even though buying things for your business can save you money come tax time, you still have to pay for them, and you will still save the most money by spending less. You can't make a profit by spending money!

The Most Common Deductions
For a list of the most common business deductions, we only have to look at IRS Schedule C, where you will report your business income and expenses. They are:

Cost of Goods Sold
The cost of goods sold is what you have paid for your raw materials or parts, the shipping cost to receive them, storage costs, and the direct labor costs to make them. Note that if you run a service business and do not sell goods, your cost of goods sold is zero.

Advertising
Any money you spend to promote your business is deductible. Examples: business cards, newspaper ads, fliers, signs.

Depreciation
Depreciation is the way your business equipment loses value over time. Rather than deduct that declining value all at once, the IRS wants you to take it over time. We'll discuss this in more detail later.

Insurance
Any expenses you have for insuring your business are deductible. Plus, if you are self-employed and the business pays your health-insurance premiums, you may be able to deduct these as well.

Legal and Professional Services
You know those lawyers and bookkeepers and accountants you are going to hire to help you? All of their fees are deductible. This category would also include other professionals such as consultants.

Office Expenses and Supplies
Included here is anything you spend to help establish and run your office, including office expenses such as chairs, tables and desks (generally, expenses are considered things that last more than a year). Office supplies such as paper, pens, and appointment books (things that generally last less than a year) are also deductible.

Repairs and Maintenance
Anything you pay to maintain or repair business equipment or property is deductible.

Note that any time you do work for your business, including repair or maintenance work, the cost of your time is never deductible. It's only if you pay someone else that you can deduct the cost of that labor. The cost of any parts or supplies is always deductible, regardless of who does the work.

Rent or Lease
If you pay someone else for the use of your business space, vehicles, machinery, or equipment, deduct that. Note that you can only claim this deduction if your business is outside of your home. If you work from home, you may be eligible for the home-office deduction, which we'll discuss later.

Taxes and Licenses
You can deduct real estate and employment taxes if you have these, as well as some other less common taxes. If your business is regulated and requires you to pay for permits, fees, or licenses, you can deduct them.

Travel, Meals, and Entertainment
Any time you travel on business, eat while on the road, or entertain clients, you can deduct the expenses. We'll discuss this in more detail later.

Utilities
Your costs for electricity, water, heat, and communications are all deductible as long as your business is outside of your home. If you work from your home, you'd use the home-office deduction instead.

Wages
What you pay to your employees, including bonuses and fringe benefits, is deductible.

What If I'm Not Sure Where My Deductions Go?
Normally it doesn't matter too much where you list your deductions on your Schedule C. With few exceptions, you get the same deduction regardless of which category you list it under. So if you accidentally list a repair under Professional Services, it probably won't matter.

Remember, as long as your business expense is "ordinary and necessary", you can deduct it.

For More Information on Business Deductions

❏ See IRS Publication 535, Business Expenses

More Common Business Deductions

Business Use of Personal Auto
Most of us own cars in our own names (as opposed to in the business name) that we use for business purposes. You can deduct the cost of using your personal auto for business purposes in one of two ways.

Standard Mileage Rate
This method of calculating your auto expense is pretty simple. You keep track of the actual miles you drive for business purposes, multiply it by the deduction the IRS sets every year, and you have your deduction. You can find current and previous year's mileage deduction by searching for "standard mileage rate" at http://www.irs.gov.

For example, let's assume that the standard mileage rate last year was 55¢. If you drove 2,344 miles that year, your total deduction would be:

2,344 miles x 0.55 = $1,289.20

We'll get to the types of records you have to keep to prove your deduction in a minute.

Actual Expense Method
Under this system, you keep track of all of your auto-related expenses—gas, tires, any repairs or parts, insurance, oil changes, and so on. Then, you calculate the percentage of your car's total mileage that was business related, and apply that percentage to your total auto expenses.

For example, if your total auto related expenses for the year were $4,567 and your percentage business mileage was 23 percent, your deductible amount would be 4,567 x .23 = $1,050.41.

Which Way Is Best?
If you use the actual expense method, you not only have to keep track of your mileage, but also all of your other auto-related expenses. For most small business owners, using the standard mileage rate gives a larger deduction with less paperwork. Of course, you are welcome to track your expenses both ways and simply take whichever gives you the largest deduction at the end of the year.

What Is a Legitimate Business Trip?
Any time you travel for ordinary and necessary business purposes, your travel is deductible. Personal trips and commuting is never deductible. For example, if you are a painter and you need to travel to a home to paint, that is deductible. However, if you have an office out of your home, travel from your home to your place of business is considered commuting, not business travel, and is not deductible.

But sometimes you can work this to your advantage. For example, going grocery shopping is not usually a business trip, but if your business bank is located near the grocery store, you can legitimately double up. The trip to the bank is deductible, and the personal part was just an add-on.

Record Keeping
Regardless of the system you choose, your records must prove that you really did use your auto for legitimate business purposes. You are required to write down the date of your business trip, the purpose of the trip or who you saw, and obviously the distance. You do not need to write down the starting and ending mileage on you odometer, unless that makes it easier for you. The IRS really, really likes you to have a written record of this.

To make things easier, always write down your mileage at the time you travel. Otherwise you'll forget, and then at the end of the year you'll try to reconstruct your business trips, forget half of them, and miss out on this legitimate deduction.

Travel, Meal, and Entertainment Costs

So let's say you start your business and decide you'd like to attend your industry's annual conference. Perhaps it's in New York, Orlando, Las Vegas, or wherever. You have to get from where you are to where it is, as well as have a place to stay and eat.

When traveling on business, all travel related expenses are 100 percent deductible. So if you take a cab to the airport, then fly to the conference city, take a bus to the hotel, and rent a car, all of those costs are deductible. So is your hotel.

Meal costs while you travel are 50 percent deductible, as are any expenses for entertaining clients or prospective customers.

What about the Family?

A question that everyone asks is, can I take a family vacation and write it all off? The answer is no, not the whole thing. But you can write off your business part of the trip. For example, let's say that you attend a three-day conference and take your family. You tack on two more days at the end just for fun.

The deduction you can take is pretty much common sense. All of your transportation costs are deductible, and your hotel and meal costs are deductible while you are attending your business conference. But the remaining days, and all of your family's expenses, are not deductible. Of course, you still save a bundle by combining business and pleasure this way; just be sure to keep good records.

Travel Records

In general, to deduct your travel and meal costs, just track the five Ws: who, what, where, when, and why.

This is actually pretty easy. Just keep receipts, because they usually have most of what you need to know. You should just make a note on the receipt of what you were doing that made this a business expense and you should be all set.

For More Information on Auto, Travel, and Meal Expenses

❏ See IRS Publication 463, Travel, Entertainment, Gift, and Car Expenses

Home-Office Deduction

In recent years, more and more businesses are being run exclusively from the business owner's home, and unlike in years past, the IRS now makes it rather easy to deduct some of the costs of having a home office. You might want to take the home-office deduction if you perform substantial work from home, regardless of whether you rent or own your home.

A home office can be used by just about any business that does not have other business space, and even some that do. For example, if you run a restaurant and have an office in the back where you do your bookkeeping, you probably can't claim the home-office deduction because you already deduct the cost of your out-of-home office. Businesses that normally perform their work out of their home, such as painters, can claim the space they use for storage and bookkeeping at home with no problem.

The Two Tests

Because the home-office deduction is so susceptible to cheating, the IRS applies two tests to see if the space you are using is really legitimate. First, they ask, is the space an ordinary and necessary place of business (where have we heard that phrase before?). Most home offices shouldn't have any trouble meeting this condition.

The second, more rigorous standard is this: Is the space for regular and exclusive business use? This means exactly what is says: The space must be used regularly for business, and only for business. The way one accountant put it to me was this: The IRS likes walls. They like to see your home office in a separate room that is used only for business.

Eliminate the Gray

Now admittedly there is some gray area here, but you want to eliminate as much of that as possible. Here are some examples of things that are clearly black and white.

A woman does fashion consulting out of her home. She has clients come in occasionally and they discuss fashion options over the dining room table. Can she take her dining room as her home office? No! The dining room is not used regularly or exclusively for business. It is used for dining, with only occasional business use. It clearly does not pass the test.

A man who lives alone has a two bedroom apartment. He sleeps in one room and has a home office set up in the other. Although there is a couch in the second bedroom, all he uses the room for is his business. Can he take the second bedroom as a home office? Clearly this situation passes the regular-and-exclusive test.

How Your Deduction Is Calculated

The IRS lets you deduct the cost of many common home expenses (discussed below) based on what percentage of your home you use for business. For example, if your home office takes up 120 square feet in a house with 1,200 square feet of living space, your percentage deductible will be

$$120 \div 1,200 = .10 \text{ or } 10\%$$

You also have to take into consideration how long you used your home office. If you started your business in July, for example, you can only take half of the expenses for the year.

What You Get to Deduct

For your home-office deduction, you can deduct both direct and indirect expenses. Direct expenses are those that affect only your home office, such as painting the room. Indirect expenses are those that apply to the entire home, such as utilities or repairs. Note that direct expenses are 100 percent deductible, while indirect expenses are only deductible as a percentage of your home used.

Things you can deduct include:

- Utilities
- Rent
- Mortgage interest
- Insurance
- Real estate taxes

Is It Worth It?

The home-office deduction sounds great, but in reality many who otherwise might be eligible for it may decide not to take it. Why? Mainly because the time required for actually keeping the records and doing the fairly complex paperwork won't justify the amount saved. Especially if you rent, the amount of money you are looking at saving could be much less than $100. You have to ask yourself if it is worth it. Of course, as with all other tax issues, if you choose to do the paperwork you can see for yourself how much you could save, and then decide for yourself.

For More Information on Home-Office Deductions

❑ See IRS Form 8829, Expenses for Business Use of Your Home

Depreciation

With most of the deductible items we've talked about so far, you are able to deduct the full value of the item right away. But for certain business property, those items with a useful life of more than one year, the IRS has you spread your deduction out over time. This is called depreciation. Typically you would depreciate things such as manufacturing equipment, buildings, vehicles, and computers. You cannot depreciate things that will never wear out, such as land, or things that are not used in your business, such as inventory.

For example, if you buy a sewing machine, you would consult a depreciation chart from the IRS to see that it would be expected to last nine years. You can chose to deduct one-ninth of its value each year, or you can elect to accelerate your depreciation. There are at least four different methods you can use to calculate how much you can depreciate every year. As you can see, what could be a simple idea can quickly become complex.

An Exception
Many small businesses would rather get their deduction sooner rather than later, especially if they are low on cash. The IRS gives you a way to take your deprecation all at once for some items using the Section 179 deduction, named for the section of the tax code it comes from. Rather than spread your deduction over time, property claimed in a Section 179 deduction can be taken all in the year the item was placed in service.

The amount of property that you can claim each year under Section 179 is at least $25,000 and varies year to year. Special laws enacted after 2001 change the limit over time, so it's best to check on the exact amount when you plan your business expenditures and taxes. In any case, the amount you can claim under Section 179 can never exceed your net profit.

Caution
When you use the Section 179 deduction, you are promising the IRS that the property will be used in your business for the number of years it would otherwise depreciate. If you dispose of your property before its normal lifetime, you are supposed to reimburse the IRS for the deduction you took.

For More Information on Depreciation

Except for pretty simple situations, depreciating property can quickly get you in over your head. This is an area that really calls for professional assistance. For more information:

❑ See IRS Publication 946, How to Depreciate Property

What Doesn't Count?

After going over this list, you might be wondering, what doesn't count as a business deduction? Almost nothing, so long as it is an ordinary and necessary business expense. But let me give you a couple of examples of things that won't count.

The IRS gives as an example of a disallowed deduction any bribes that you have paid as part of your business. They may be expected in your line of work, but they are not deductible.

Another one you might hear is that if you buy a sign for your car, perhaps one of those magnetic signs that you attach to your car doors, you can deduct the entire cost of the car. After all, isn't it now really a rolling billboard? Well, no. There are ways to deduct some of the costs of using your car in business, but this isn't one of them. The cost of the sign is certainly deducible, but not the entire car it is attached to.

RECORD KEEPING

For better or worse, you are ultimately responsible for calculating the correct amount of tax to pay. This means that if the IRS believes you might have made a mistake, it is up to you to prove you are right, not for them to prove you are wrong.

Therefore, you want to keep excellent records. This will not only help if you are audited by allowing you to demonstrate that your tax calculations were correct, but also because keeping good records reduces the chances of being audited in the first place.

What to Keep

In addition to the summaries of your financial transactions that you will keep in your checkbook register, income-and-expense journals or ledgers, and financial statements, you should also keep the original supporting or source documents that are generated when you do business.

These are simply the documents that you create or receive when you sell goods, buy items to resell, or purchase items for use in your business. Some examples of supporting documents include:

- Cash register tapes and receipts
- Bank deposit slips
- Credit card charge slips
- Invoices, both sent and received
- Any type of receipt
- Inventory records
- Copies of your filed tax returns

How Long to Keep Records

Each state has different laws for how long you have to keep supporting records. These laws may be longer or shorter than the federal requirements.

For most situations, the IRS requires you to keep to keep records for three years, although this may vary depending on the circumstances. If you depreciate property, you must keep the paperwork for that property as long as you depreciate it. Plus, it is possible that creditors or your insurance company may want you to keep these records longer than the IRS requires.

If for some reason you failed to file a tax return or filed a fraudulent return, there is no limit on the period of time the IRS can ask you for supporting documents. Even if you have always filed correct returns, you should keep copies of the returns themselves forever (only the return itself is required, not the supporting documents).

Many experts recommend that you keep paperwork for seven years, as this is longer than most states require. A good rule of thumb for record keeping: Keep as much as you can for as long as you can.

For More Information on Record Keeping

❑ See IRS Publication 583, Starting a Business and Keeping Records

NAIL IT DOWN!

Here are the key elements to remember in when it comes to keeping your taxes as low as possible.

Tax Basics

❑ Want to pay zero taxes? Easy! Make no money!

❑ Successful businesses will get expert tax advice.

❑ Have a bookkeeping system in place and ready to go before you start business to make your first year's taxes as painless as possible.

❑ Get an EIN.

❑ Get any state or local permits and numbers before making sales, and find out if your state or local government require you to collect and remit sales tax.

❑ If you are making a profit, don't forget to file estimated taxes as you go to the IRS; your state may require them as well.

❑ Estimated taxes are used to fulfill your income and self-employment tax obligations.

❑ Self-employment taxes are for your Social Security and Medicare taxes.

❑ If you have employees, you will be responsible for withholding and remitting their payroll taxes (get expert advice!).

Tax Returns

❑ Simpler businesses have simpler tax returns.

❑ Sole proprietors and single-member LLCs will do their taxes the same way in most cases.

❑ Filing a tax return is almost always in your interest, even if it is not required.

❑ The basic forms for many businesses are:

    ❑ Schedule C, for reporting business income and expenses.

    ❑ Schedule SE, for calculating self-employment tax due.

    ❑ Form 1040, for bringing it all together and calculating total tax due.

Deductions

❑ All ordinary and necessary business expenses are considered deductible from your business income, and thus reduce your taxes.

❑ Business deductions save you at tax time, but you still have the expense. The best way to increase profit is to decrease expenses.

❑ Common deductions include:

    ❑ Advertising

    ❑ Depreciation

    ❑ Insurance

    ❑ Legal and professional services

❑ Other common deductions include:

    ❑ Business use of personal auto

    ❑ Home-office deduction

    ❑ Business travel and meals

Record Keeping

❑ In general, you should keep records:

    ❑ Of as much as you can

    ❑ For as long as you can

    ❑ Keep copies of tax returns forever

Contacting the IRS

❑ 1-800-829-3676

❑ http://www.irs.gov

❑ For more specific small business issues, go to: http://www.irs.gov/businesses/small/

Helpful IRS Publications

- ❑ Publication 583, Starting a Business and Keeping Records

- ❑ Publication 334, Tax Guide for Small Business

- ❑ Publication 463, Travel, Entertainment, Gift, and Car Expenses

- ❑ Publication 533, Self-Employment Tax

- ❑ Publication 1635, Understanding Your EIN

- ❑ Publication 505, Tax Withholding and Estimated Taxes

- ❑ IRS Form 1040-ES, Estimated Taxes for Individuals

- ❑ Publication 535, Business Expenses

- ❑ Publication 587, Business Use of Your Home

- ❑ Publication 946, How to Depreciate Property

- ❑ Publication 541, Partnerships

- ❑ Publication 15, Employer's Tax Guide

Chapter Sixteen

KNOW HOW TO WRITE A BUSINESS PLAN

Congratulations on finishing this book! You have shown that you are serious about self-employment, and you now know more about running a business that at least 80 percent of your competition. If you are still serious about starting your business, you have two more very important tasks ahead.

MAKING THE BEST DECISION FOR YOU

Remember back in chapter 1, *Know Yourself and Your Business*, I said that there were three decisions you could make when you completed the book. These were:

- To go ahead with your business idea.

- To put off starting a business until you were more prepared.

- To realize that running a business wasn't for you.

Hopefully you are even more enthusiastic about your business idea than you were when you started. Or, you may now realize that there is more to running a business than you thought, and you'll need some more education, experience, or training before you are ready to start your business. In either case, you definitely want to check out the rest of this chapter.

On the other hand, you may have discovered that running a business is more work than you had hoped, or perhaps you're just not up to it. If this is your decision, you are to be congratulated! Part of my goal in creating this book was to help you make the best decision you can make, and if that is to not start a business, then I have succeeded.

Why Write a Business Plan?

For many business owners, the key to starting a successful business is first creating a written business plan. A business plan is a document that describes, in some detail, exactly what the business is, how it will run, and why it will be successful. Think of it as your business's blueprint. Just as you wouldn't attempt to build a house without a blueprint, you probably shouldn't attempt to build a business without a business plan.

There are a lot of good reasons to write a business plan:

- A business plan lets you clarify your ideas on paper before you actually carry them out. Business plans are great for focusing your ideas on what is important.

- It lets you show, not just tell, others about the business you want to build.

- It lets you experiment on paper, so that you can avoid mistakes and discover ahead of time if there are any missing parts.

- If you need a loan to help get your business off the ground, it will help sell your business idea to a lender. Just as no bank would lend you money for a house without a blueprint, no reputable lender will provide capital for a business without a business plan.

Starting and running a business will force you to make many decisions and answer many questions. Just as it would be difficult to decide how large you wanted your house to be as it was being built, it can be tough to make informed decisions for your business once it is up and running. Business plans force you to consider, research, and answer these questions ahead of time, so that when the issues arise for real, you'll be prepared.

This chapter is designed to help you learn what you'll be in for when it comes to building your plan. Chances are that you already have most of the skills required to construct your own business plan. However, writing a business plan, especially one that will be considered by a lender, isn't easy, and you should look for any help you can get. I would encourage you to seek out many sources of information, such as books, libraries, websites, and your local SCORE, SBA, and SBDC offices.

Business Plan Options

You have several options for assistance when it comes to writing a business plan.

Pay Someone to Do It

This option is great if you can afford it. Creating a business plan from scratch is hard work, and expensive if you pay someone else to do it. Plan on around $1,000 to $2,000 for a simple business plan, $3,000 to $10,000 for complex businesses.

Buy a Software Planning Guide

Software guides promise you that can just enter the details and it will fill in the routine text. Unfortunately, the resulting plans tend to read like they were written by computer. Nothing can replace your voice in creating a plan. Plus, software computer guides have many of the same advantages and disadvantages that we saw with computerized bookkeeping systems: If you don't know what is going on behind the scenes, you may be surprised at the result.

Use a Business-Plan Book

Business-plan books have the advantage that they don't do any of the writing for you, rather they guide you through writing your own plan. There are several excellent ones available.

Let's look at some of the topics covered in a business plan and some of the questions you'll be expected to consider.

ELEMENTS OF A BUSINESS PLAN

Because the goal of the business plan is to force you to think about and explain your plan, all business plans cover the same topics. However, not all business plans call their topics by the same name or present them in the exact same order. This section presents the topics in the order that makes the most sense, starting with the broadest, most general topics and becoming more and more specific, reflecting your research and knowledge. Your actual business plan will require you to be much more specific and require a great deal more detail than this chapter covers.

You will write the sections of the plan in the same order as they will be presented in the plan itself, with one exception —one of the last things you will write is your executive summary, a topic that goes in the front of the plan. The reason is simple: You can't summarize what you haven't written.

Executive Summary

The executive summary is usually a one to two page summary of the entire plan. It fulfills two major purposes.

First, it summarizes the entire plan. It will briefly describe the business itself, your market analysis and competition research, your marketing and promotional ideas, your operations and management plans, and your financial position. It's the whole plan on one page.

Second, it serves as an invitation and incentive to read the rest of the plan. Typically no one is going to read your entire plan unless he or she is interested in it to begin with. And the way you spark his or her curiosity is by creating an executive summary that makes him or her want to read more.

Business Description

The business description section of your business plan helps answer some of the nitty-gritty questions about the details of your business. Someone who has only dreamed of running a business can briefly explain a business idea, but only someone who is serious and spent a lot of time thinking about his or her idea can write a good business description. If you haven't spent that time yet, use this opportunity to translate your mission into details.

In general, the business description explains the business idea in some detail, including why the owner is qualified to run the business, who the customers are, and why the business will succeed.

Questions:

❑ What is your product or service?

❑ What industry are you in?

❑ What is it about your product that will make customers like it?

❑ Who are your customers?

❑ What are the goals of your business?

❑ Why will a customer buy from you rather than the competition?

Market Analysis

A market analysis looks at three factors that will have a major impact on your business success:

- the industry your business is in;
- the market, or potential customers you may have;
- and your competition.

You should be able to research your market effectively enough to convince the reader that you are aware of market trends, that there is a healthy demand for your product, and that you can successfully distinguish yourself from your competition.

Questions:

❑ What desire does your customer have that your product can fulfill?

❑ What are the trends in your industry?

❑ Who are the major players in your industry?

❑ What are your customer's demographics? How do you know?

❑ How often would a customer buy from you?

❑ How will you use the elements of price, quality, and service to distinguish your product?

❑ Who are your main competitors? What are their strengths and weaknesses?

❑ How will you ensure quality?

Marketing Plan

Performing market research should give you a solid background into your customers and competitors. But market research is just the first step. Your knowing that a market exists isn't the same as the market knowing you exist!

To let your market know that you exist involves another step: marketing. As I explained in chapter 10, marketing means two things—to let your potential customers know that you exist and to keep the customers you already have. Every business must take these steps, because no customers will buy from you if they don't know how your business can fulfill their needs.

Often when people hear the word "marketing," the first thing they think of is advertising. Advertising is a form of marketing, but the types of marketing you'll do will depend on how much money you have, the type of business you are in, and who your customers are. No marketing plan is complete without a marketing budget that establishes how much money you can afford to spend on this essential task.

Don't have much money? Then be prepared to spend a lot of time personally promoting your business. If you don't get out there and sing the praises of your product, who will?

Questions:

❑ How do you want customers to view your business?

❑ What features and benefits does your product have? How do they compare to the competition's?

☐ How will you distribute your product to your customers?

☐ How will you promote your product?

☐ How much money do you have to spend on promotion?

Management and Operations

The management and operations section of your business plan requires you to explain in some detail exactly how you will operate the business. For example, if you manufacture a product, you should be able to explain your supply chain: how much you will pay for parts or raw materials, the process you go through to create your finished product, and how your product is packaged and distributed. If you run a service business, you should be able to explain how customers will contact you, your hours of operation, and where and how you will see customers. In all cases you should have a handle on the following questions.

Questions:

☐ What business experience do you have?

☐ How do your education, training, and experience qualify you to run this business?

☐ Will you run the business alone or with others? If you have partners, do you have a written partnership agreement?

☐ Do you have any barriers to success? If so, how will you get around them?

❑ What is the process you use to manufacture or create your product?

❑ Do you need any permits or licenses for your business?

Financial Projections

Your business plan now gets to where the rubber meets the road: money. If you are like most business owners, chances are you want to make money, the more the better. Yet many businesses can't stay in business because they can't pay their bills. Everyone imagines that, once his or her business starts, the cash will just flow in. But the real world is usually a lot more difficult than that. You'll have to work hard to earn that money.

Your financial projections will explain in detail exactly how you expect your business finances will look for the next several years. You will explain:

- what financial assumptions you are making regarding your costs, expenses, and income;
- where the money will come from to start your business;
- what your breakeven sales and price will be;
- how you will determine the price of your product;
- and whether you need a loan to get started, and if so, how you will pay it back.

These financial projections are presented in the form of the three most common financial statements: the cash flow, profit and loss, and balance sheet. One of the skills all business owners should have is the knowledge of what these statements are and how they reflect the financial condition of their business.

Chapter 14, *Know Accounting Basics*, has a good summary of what goes into your financials and what lenders look for in solid financial projections.

NAIL IT DOWN!

As we mentioned at the start of this chapter, a business plan is only one of the elements to getting a successful business off the ground. To help you with planning, here is a basic checklist to help you get an idea of what steps most businesses will have to take to get up and running. This is a basic list; in reality there will be hundreds of steps you will have to take, and this is just an outline.

Note that a business plan is at the start of the list. Having a plan before you start your business will help ensure that you do not take one step back for every two steps forward.

Basic Startup Checklist

❑ Develop a business plan.

❑ Prepare all the necessary legal documents, as applicable. Complete paperwork for your entity:

   ❑ LLC

   ❑ Partnership

   ❑ Corporation

   Obtain tax forms:

   ❑ Federal taxpayer identification number (SS-4, IRS)

   ❑ State seller's and tax ID permit

❑ Estimated taxes (Form 1040-ES)

❑ Industry specific licenses

❑ Open a business checking account, and select and implement a financial record-keeping system.

❑ Purchase adequate insurance.

❑ Find a location for the business:

❑ Check zoning requirements.

❑ Negotiate a lease if outside the home.

❑ Design the layout of the business.

❑ Arrange for phone service.

❑ Promote the business in following your marketing plan.

❑ If hiring employees:

❑ Prepare job descriptions.

❑ Advertise, interview, hire, and train applicants.

❑ Write policy manual.

❑ Order supplies such as business cards, stationary, and checks.

❑ Ongoing operations:

❑ Prepare quarterly payroll returns and pay estimated taxes.

❑ Prepare monthly or quarterly financial statements.

❑ Join industry associations and groups.

Index

Books from Allworth Press

Allworth Press is an imprint of Skyhorse Publishing, Inc. Selected titles are listed below

---

The Pocket Small Business Owner's Guide to Negotiating
by Richard Weisgrau (5 ½ x 8 ¼, 224 pages, paperback, $14.95)

The Entrepreneurial Age
by Larry C. Farrell (6 x 9, 256 pages, paperback, $27.50)

The Pocket Legal Companion to Trademark: A User-Friendly Handbook on Avoiding Lawsuits and Protecting Your Trademarks
by Lee Wilson (5 x 7½, 320 pages, paperback, $16.95)

The Pocket Legal Companion to Copyright: A User-Friendly Handbook for Profiting from Copyrights
by Lee Wilson (5 x 7½, 320 pages, paperback, $16.95)

Emotional Branding, Revised Edition: The New Paradigm for Connecting Brands to People
by Marc Gobe (6 x 9, 344 pages, paperback, $24.95)

The Art of Digital Branding, Revised Edition
by Ian Cocoran (6 x 9, 272 pages, paperback, $23.95)

Turn Your Idea or Invention into Millions
by Don Kracke (6 x 9, 224 pages, paperback, $18.95)

Legal Forms for Everyone, Fifth Edition
by Carl W. Battle (8 ½ x 11, 240 pages, paperback, $24.95)

Your Living Trust and Estate Plan, 2012–2013: How to Maximize Your Family's Assets and Protect Your Loved Ones
by Harvey J. Platt (6 x 9, 352 pages, paperback, $23.95)

Power Speaking: The Art of the Exceptional Public Speaker
by Achim Nowak (6 x 9, 256 pages, paperback, $19.95)

To see our complete catalog or to order online, please visit *www.allworth.com.*